BOLSTERING THE GOVERNMENT'S CYBERSECURITY: LESSONS LEARNED FROM WANNACRY

JOINT HEARING

BEFORE THE

SUBCOMMITTEE ON OVERSIGHT & SUBCOMMITTEE ON RESEARCH AND TECHNOLOGY

COMMITTEE ON SCIENCE, SPACE, AND TECHNOLOGY

HOUSE OF REPRESENTATIVES

ONE HUNDRED FIFTEENTH CONGRESS

FIRST SESSION

___

June 15, 2017

___

Serial No. 115–17

___

Printed for the use of the Committee on Science, Space, and Technology

Available via the World Wide Web: http://science.house.gov

___

U.S. GOVERNMENT PUBLISHING OFFICE

26–234PDF   WASHINGTON : 2017

For sale by the Superintendent of Documents, U.S. Government Publishing Office
Internet: bookstore.gpo.gov   Phone: toll free (866) 512–1800; DC area (202) 512–1800
Fax: (202) 512–2104   Mail: Stop IDCC, Washington, DC 20402–0001

CONTENTS

June 15, 2017

Appendix II: Additional Material for the Record

BOLSTERING THE GOVERNMENT'S CYBERSECURITY: LESSONS LEARNED FROM WANNACRY

Thursday, June 15, 2017

House of Representatives,
Subcommittee on Oversight and
Subcommittee on Research and Technology
Committee on Science, Space, and Technology,
Washington, D.C.

The Subcommittees met, pursuant to call, at 10:05 a.m., in Room 2318 of the Rayburn House Office Building, Hon. Darin LaHood [Chairman of the Subcommittee on Oversight] presiding.

LAMAR S. SMITH, Texas
CHAIRMAN

EDDIE BERNICE JOHNSON, Texas
RANKING MEMBER

Congress of the United States
House of Representatives

COMMITTEE ON SCIENCE, SPACE, AND TECHNOLOGY

2321 RAYBURN HOUSE OFFICE BUILDING

WASHINGTON, DC 20515-6301

(202) 225-6371

www.science.house.gov

Subcommittees on Oversight and Research and Technology

Bolstering the Government's Cybersecurity: Lessons Learned from WannaCry

Thursday, June 15, 2017
10:00 a.m. – 12:00 p.m.
2318 Rayburn House Office Building

Witnesses

Mr. Salim Neino, Chief Executive Officer, Kryptos Logic

Dr. Charles H. Romine, Director, Information Technology Laboratory, National Institute of Standards and Technology

Mr. Gregory J. Touhill, CISSP, CISM; Brigadier General, USAF (ret); Adjunct Professor, Cybersecurity & Risk Management, Carnegie Mellon University, Heinz College

Dr. Hugh Thompson, Chief Technology Officer, Symantec

U.S. HOUSE OF REPRESENTATIVES
COMMITTEE ON SCIENCE, SPACE, AND TECHNOLOGY

HEARING CHARTER

Thursday, June 8, 2017

TO: Members, Committee on Science, Space, and Technology

FROM: Majority Staff, Committee on Science, Space, and Technology

SUBJECT: Oversight Subcommittee and Research and Technology Subcommittee hearing: "Bolstering the Government's Cybersecurity: Lessons Learned from WannaCry"

The Subcommittee on Oversight and the Subcommittee on Research and Technology of the Committee on Science, Space, and Technology will hold a joint hearing titled *Bolstering the Government's Cybersecurity: Lessons Learned from WannaCry* on Thursday, June 15, 2017, at 10:00 a.m. in Room 2318 of the Rayburn House Office Building.

Hearing Purpose

The purpose of the hearing is to examine the recent WannaCry ransomware attack that compromised computer systems globally last month. Because the ransomware attack was the first of its kind, the hearing will allow Members to hear recommendations for what the government can do to ensure its systems are protected against similar and possibly more sophisticated attacks. The hearing will also examine the benefits of public-private partnerships for cybersecurity, as well as the President's recent Executive Order, which makes NIST's Cybersecurity Framework mandatory for Executive Branch departments and agencies.

Witness List

- **Mr. Salim Neino**, Chief Executive Officer, Kryptos Logic
- **Dr. Charles H. Romine**, Director, Information Technology Laboratory, National Institute of Standards and Technology
- **Mr. Gregory J. Touhill**, CISSP, CISM; Brigadier General, USAF (ret); Adjunct Professor, Cybersecurity & Risk Management, Carnegie Mellon University, Heinz College
- **Dr. Hugh Thompson**, Chief Technology Officer, Symantec

Staff Contact

For questions related to the hearing, please contact Caroline Ingram of the Majority Staff at 202-225-6371.

4

Chairman LaHood. The Subcommittee on Oversight and the Subcommittee on Research and Technology will come to order.

Without objection, the Chair is authorized to declare a recess of the Subcommittee at any time.

Good morning, and welcome to today's hearing titled "Bolstering the Government's Cybersecurity: Lessons Learned from WannaCry." I recognize myself for five minutes for an opening statement.

I want to welcome the witnesses here today, and I would also welcome Chairman Smith, Oversight Subcommittee Ranking Member Beyer, Research and Technology Subcommittee Vice Chairman Abraham, Research and Technology Ranking Member Lipinski, Members of the Subcommittees, our expert witnesses, and members of the audience.

Cybersecurity—a concept we hear mentioned frequently, especially in this period of rapidly emerging threats—is an ever-evolving concept. Maintaining an effective cybersecurity posture requires constant vigilance as new threats emerge and old ones return. Too often, however, when we hear about the importance of cybersecurity, we are left without concrete steps to take to ensure our systems are best positioned to defend against emerging threats.

One of the goals of today's hearing is to learn about real, tangible measures the government can take to ensure its IT security systems are appropriately reinforced to defend against new and emerging threats, including novel and sophisticated ransomware threats.

The specific focus of today's hearing will be the recent WannaCry ransomware attack, a new type of ransomware infection, which affected over one million unique systems last month in a worldwide attack that impacted nearly every country in the world.

Although the concept of ransomware is not new, the type of ransomware employed by WannaCry was novel. WannaCry worked by encrypting documents on a computer, instructing victims to pay $300 in Bitcoin in order to regain access to their user's documents. Unlike typical forms of ransomware, however, WannaCry signaled the ushering in of a new type of worming ransomware, which caused the attack to spread faster and more rapidly with each new infection.

In light of the novelty built into WannaCry's method of attack, cybersecurity experts, including those we will hear from today, have expressed significant concerns that WannaCry is only a preview of a more sophisticated ransomware infection that many believe will inevitably be launched by hackers in the near future.

Beginning May 12, 2017, the WannaCry ransomware infection moved rapidly across Asia and Europe, eventually hitting the United States. The attack infected 7,000 computers in the first hour and 110,000 distinct IP addresses in 2 days and in almost 100 countries, including the U.K., Russia, China, Ukraine, and India. Experts now believe WannaCry affected approximately 1 to 2 million unique systems worldwide prior to activating the kill switch.

In Illinois, my home state, Cook County's IT systems were compromised by WannaCry, reportedly one of a few local governments subject to the attack. Although Cook County has worked to appropriately patch their systems, it is important that we ensure that all vulnerabilities are appropriately remedied in the event of a more sophisticated attack.

Fortunately, the hackers responsible for WannaCry mistakenly included a kill switch, which was uncovered by an employee of Kryptos Logic and used to terminate the attack. The Kryptos Logic employee exploited a key mistake made by the hackers when he registered the domain connected to the ransomware attack. Experts estimate that the kill switch prevented 10 to 15 million unique worldwide system infections and reinfections.

Although based on information available thus far the federal government's systems were fortunately spared from WannaCry, we want to ensure that the government is sufficiently prepared in the likely event of a more sophisticated attack.

Additionally, the Committee wants to hear what Congress can do to appropriately address this Committee—I'm sorry—this climate of new and improving cybersecurity threats.

Through the lens of the aftermath of WannaCry, today's witnesses will help shed light on key steps the government should take to ensure its systems are protected. We will also hear today about how public-private partnerships are an instrumental tool to help bolster the government's cybersecurity posture. Finally, we will learn about how the President's recent cybersecurity order, which makes NIST's cybersecurity framework mandatory on the Executive Branch, is a significant step toward ensuring the federal government's cybersecurity posture incorporates the most innovative security measures to defend against evolving threats.

It is my hope that our discussions here today will highlight areas where improvement is necessary, while offering recommendations as we move forward to ensure the federal government is prepared to respond to emerging cybersecurity threats. I look forward to hearing from our distinguished witnesses.

[The prepared statement of Chairman LaHood follows:]

For Immediate Release
June 15, 2017

Media Contact: Kristina Baum
(202) 225-6371

Statement of Chairman Darin LaHood (R-Ill.)

Bolstering the Government's Cybersecurity: Lessons Learned from WannaCry

Chairman LaHood: Good morning and welcome to today's joint subcommittee hearing: "Bolstering the Government's Cybersecurity: Lessons Learned from WannaCry."

I would like to welcome Chairman Smith, Oversight Subcommittee Ranking Member Beyer, Research and Technology Subcommittee Chairman Abraham, Research and Technology Ranking Member Lipinski, Members of the Subcommittees, our expert witnesses, and members of the audience.

Cybersecurity—a concept we hear mentioned frequently, especially in this period of rapidly emerging threats—is an ever-evolving concept. Maintaining an effective cybersecurity posture requires constant vigilance as new threats emerge and old ones return. Too often, however, when we hear about the importance of cybersecurity we are left without concrete steps to take to ensure our systems are best positioned to defend against emerging threats. One of the goals of today's hearing is to learn about real, tangible measures the government can take to ensure its IT security systems are appropriately reinforced to defend against new and emerging threats, including novel and sophisticated ransomware threats.

The specific focus of today's hearing will be the recent WannaCry ransomware attack, a new type of ransomware infection, which affected over one million unique systems last month in a worldwide attack that impacted nearly every country in the world.

Although the concept of ransomware is not new, the type of ransomware employed by WannaCry was novel. WannaCry worked by encrypting documents on a computer, instructing victims to pay $300 in bitcoin in order to regain access to the user's documents. Unlike typical forms of ransomware, however, WannaCry signaled the ushering in of a new type of "worming" ransomware, which caused the attack to spread faster and more rapidly with each new infection. In light of the novelty built into WannaCry's method of attack, cybersecurity experts, including those we will hear from today, have expressed significant concerns that WannaCry is only a preview of a more sophisticated ransomware infection that many believe will inevitably be launched by hackers in the near future.

Beginning May 12, 2017, the WannaCry ransomware infection moved rapidly across Asia and Europe, eventually hitting the United States. The attack infected 7,000 computers in the first hour and 110,000 distinct IP addresses in two days and in almost 100 countries, including the U.K., Russia, China, Ukraine, and India. Experts now believe WannaCry affected approximately 1 to 2 million unique systems worldwide prior to activating the kill switch.

Close to my district, Cook County's IT systems were compromised by WannaCry—reportedly one of a few local governments subject to the attack. Although Cook County has worked to appropriately patch their systems, it is important that we ensure that all vulnerabilities are appropriately remedied in the event of a more sophisticated attack.

Fortunately, the hackers responsible for WannaCry mistakenly included a kill switch, which was uncovered by an employee of Kryptos Logic and used to terminate the attack. The Kryptos Logic employee exploited a key mistake made by the hackers when he registered the domain connected to the ransomware attack. Experts estimate that the kill switch prevented 10 to 15 million unique worldwide systems infections and reinfections.

Although based on information available thus far the federal government's systems were fortunately spared from WannaCry, we want to ensure that the government is sufficiently prepared in the likely event of a more sophisticated attack. Additionally, the Committee wants to hear what Congress can do to appropriately address this climate of new and emerging cybersecurity threats.

Through the lens of the aftermath of WannaCry, today's witnesses will help shed light on key steps the government should take to ensure its systems are protected. We will also hear today about how public-private partnerships are an instrumental tool to help bolster the government's cybersecurity posture. Finally, we will learn about how the President's recent cybersecurity order, which makes NIST's cybersecurity framework mandatory on the Executive Branch, is a significant step toward ensuring the federal government's cybersecurity posture incorporates the most innovative security measures to defend against evolving threats.

It is my hope that our discussions here today will highlight areas where improvement is necessary, while offering recommendations as we move forward to ensure the federal government is prepared to respond to emerging cybersecurity threats. I look forward to hearing from our distinguished witnesses.

###

Chairman LaHood. I now recognize the Ranking Member of the Oversight Subcommittee, Mr. Beyer, for an opening statement.

Mr. Beyer. Thank you very much, Mr. Chairman. I'd like to thank you and Chairman Comstock for holding this hearing.

Cybersecurity should be a chief concern for every government, business, and private citizen. In 2014, the Office of Personnel Management's information security systems, and two of the systems used by OPM contractors, were breached by state-sponsored hackers, compromising the personal information of millions of Americans. That same year, hackers released the personal information of Sony Pictures executives, embarrassing e-mails between Sony Pictures employees, and even copies of then-unreleased Sony movies. In 2015, hackers also took control of the power grid in western Ukraine and shut off power for over 200,000 residents. These three quick examples show the varied and widespread effects of cybersecurity breaches.

So we know the cybersecurity breach that was the genesis for this hearing was the WannaCry outbreak. WannaCry ransomware infected at least 300,000 computers worldwide, and could have been much worse, so I want to thank CEO Neino, head of Kryptos Logic, for being wise enough to find an employee who found that kill switch, unless you did it yourself. And we're very lucky that that was found quickly, and we are fortunate that federal systems were resistant to WannaCry. But we know we may not be as lucky the next time. We must continue to strengthen our cybersecurity posture.

By the way, in preparing for this, I've learned from our wonderful staff that I really need to upload our security upgrades every time we get a chance on our personal computers and on our smartphones.

The May 11th Executive Order on strengthening the cybersecurity of federal networks seeks to build on the Obama Administration's successes in the cybersecurity arena, and I'm happy that the Trump Administration—I don't agree with them on every topic—but they've taken this next good step. The Executive Order calls for a host of actions and a myriad of reports on federal cybersecurity from every government agency.

Simultaneously, the Trump Administration has been slow to fill newly vacant positions in nearly every government agency, and my concern is that understaffed agencies are going to have significant difficulty meeting the dictates of the Executive Order. Frankly, I'm also concerned that proposed budget cuts in the original Trump-Mulvaney budget across all agencies will make the task a lot harder to strengthen the security of federal information systems. We've got to make sure that the federal government has the resources and staffing to meet the need in this vital area.

The Executive Order also calls for agencies to begin using the NIST Framework for cybersecurity efforts, and I'm glad that we have NIST here with us today. They play a very important role in setting cybersecurity standards that could help thwart and impede cyber-attacks.

You know, NIST is world renowned for its expertise in standards development, and federal agencies will be well served by using the NIST Framework. On a precautionary note, though, I believe some efforts to expand NIST's cybersecurity role beyond their current mission and expertise are well intentioned but perhaps misplaced. We recently had a debate of H.R. 1224 here, the "NIST Cybersecurity Framework, Assessment, and Auditing Act of 2017," which gives NIST auditing authority for all federal civilian information systems. Currently, this is a responsibility of the Inspector Generals at each agency. They have the statutory authority, the experience, the expertise. They respond directly, responsible to Congress. NIST has no such experience or expertise, and I at least remain concerned about this proposal, and I'd be interested in any of the expert witnesses' thoughts on NIST's role in cybersecurity and auditing.

So I look forward to hearing from all of you today. I especially look forward to hearing from our General, the former federal CISO, about his experience in these positions and thoughts.

One final note. Bloomberg reported this week that the Russian meddling in our electoral system was far worse than what's been previously reported. According to the report, hackers attempted to delete or alter voter data, accessed software designed to be used by poll workers, and, in at least one instance, accessed a campaign finance database. These efforts didn't need to change individual votes in order to influence the election, and we really should take these sorts of cyber threats very seriously. I think Vice President Cheney called this a war on our democracy.

So Mr. Chairman, this Committee held more than a half dozen hearings on cybersecurity issues during the last Congress, including one on protecting the 2016 elections from cyber and voting machine attacks, so given what we now know about the hacking and meddling in 2016, I hope that this hearing today will be a precursor to more hearings on how we can better protect our voting systems.

Mr. Chairman, thank you so much, and I yield back.

[The prepared statement of Mr. Beyer follows:]

<u>OPENING STATEMENT</u>
Ranking Member Don Beyer (D-VA)
of the Subcommittee on Oversight

Committee on Science, Space, and Technology
Subcommittee on Oversight
Subcommittee on Research and Technology
"Bolstering the Government's Cybersecurity: Lessons Learned from WannaCry,"
June 15, 2017

Thank you Chairman LaHood and Chairman Comstock.

Cybersecurity should be a chief concern for every government, business, and private citizen.

In 2014, the Office of Personnel Management's (OPM) information security systems, and two of the systems used by OPM contractors, were breached by state-sponsored hackers, compromising the personal information of millions of Americans. That same year, hackers released the personal information of Sony Pictures executives, embarrassing e-mails between Sony Pictures employees, and even copies of then-unreleased Sony movies. In 2015, hackers also took control of the power grid in western Ukraine and shut off power for over 200,000 residents. These three quick examples show the varied and widespread effects of cybersecurity breaches.

The cybersecurity issue that was the genesis for this hearing was the WannaCry outbreak of last month. WannaCry ransomware infected over 300,000 computers worldwide, and could have been much worse. Fortunately, a "kill switch" was quickly found and deployed by an employee of Kryptos Logic—whose CEO, Mr. Neino is joining us today. We were lucky that a solution was found quickly, and we are fortunate that federal systems were resistant to WannaCry. But we know we may not be as lucky with the next threat. We must continue to strengthen our cybersecurity posture.

The May 11th Executive Order on "Strengthening the Cybersecurity of Federal Networks" seeks to build on the Obama administration's successes in the cybersecurity arena, and I am happy that this Administration, with which I disagree on most topics, has taken this next step. The Executive Order calls for a host of actions and a myriad of reports on federal cybersecurity from every government agency. Simultaneously, the Trump Administration has been slow to fill newly vacant positions in nearly every government agency. My concern is that understaffed agencies will have significant difficulty meeting the dictates of the Executive Order. I'm also concerned that proposed budget cuts across the agencies, if enacted, will make the task of strengthening the security of Federal information systems that much harder. We must insure that government has the resources and staffing to meet the need in this vital area.

The Executive Order also calls for agencies to begin using the NIST Framework for its cybersecurity efforts. NIST plays a very important role in setting cybersecurity standards that can help thwart and impede cyber-attacks. NIST is world renowned for its expertise in standards development. Federal agencies will be well served by using the NIST Framework.

However, as a precautionary note, I believe some efforts to expand NIST's cybersecurity role beyond their current mission and expertise are well intentioned but misplaced. For example, our Committee recently debated H.R. 1224, the "NIST Cybersecurity Framework, Assessment, and Auditing Act of 2017," which gives NIST auditing authority for all Federal civilian information systems. Currently, the Offices of Inspector General at each agency have the statutory authority, as well as the experience and expertise to conduct cybersecurity audits for their respective agencies. NIST has no such experience or expertise. I remain concerned about this proposal and I would be interested in any of our expert witnesses' thoughts on NIST's role in cybersecurity. But, regardless of where this important mission is placed, the Government must establish proper levels of staffing and resources. That financial reality must be addressed.

I look forward to hearing from all of today's witnesses about best cybersecurity practices of the federal government and ways for the government to improve its cybersecurity posture. I look forward to hearing from Gen. Gregory Touhill, former Federal CISO, about his experience in that positions and thoughts on the way forward for federal cybersecurity policy.

One final note, Bloomberg reported this week that the Russian meddling in our electoral system was far worse than what has been previously reported. According to the report, hackers attempted to delete or alter voter data, accessed software designed to be used by poll workers, and, in at least one instance, accessed a campaign finance database. These efforts did not need to change individual votes in order to influence the election, and we should take these sorts of cyber threats very seriously.

Mr. Chairman, this Committee held more than a half dozen hearings on cybersecurity issues during the last Congress, including one titled: Protecting the 2016 Elections from Cyber and Voting Machine Attacks. Given what we now know about hacking and meddling in the 2016 election, I hope that this hearing today will be followed up with a hearing to examine how we can better protect our voting systems.

Thank you Mr. Chairman. I yield back.

Chairman LaHood. Thank you, Mr. Beyer, for your opening statement.

I now recognize the Vice Chair of the Research and Technology Subcommittee, Mr. Abraham, for an opening statement.

Mr. Abraham. Thank you, Mr. Chairman.

Over the last few years, we've seen an alarming increase in the number and intensity of our cyber-attacks. These attacks by cyber criminals and by unfriendly governments have compromised the personal information of millions of Americans, jeopardized thousands of our businesses and their employees, and threatened interruption of critical public services.

The recent WannaCry ransomware attack demonstrates that cyber-attacks are continuing to go from bad to worse. This most recent large-scale cyber-attack affected more than one to two million systems in more than 190 countries. Nevertheless, it appears that the impact could have been much more catastrophic considering how fast that ransomware spread.

And while organizations and individuals within the United States were largely unscathed, due in part to a security researcher identifying a web-based "kill switch," the potential destructiveness of WannaCry warns us to expect similar attacks in the future. Before those attacks happen, we need to make sure that our information systems are very ready.

During a Research and Technology Subcommittee hearing earlier this year, a witness representing the U.S. Government Accountability Office—the GAO—testified, and I quote, "Over the past several years, GAO has made about 2,500 recommendations to federal agencies to enhance their information security programs and controls. As of February 2017, about 1,000 recommendations had not been implemented."

It is clear that the status quo in federal government cyber security is a virtual invitation for more cyber-attacks. We must take strong steps in order to properly secure our systems and databases before another cyber-attack like WannaCry happens and puts our government up for ransom.

On March 1, 2017, this Committee approved H.R. 1224, the NIST Cybersecurity Framework, Assessment, and Auditing Act of 2017, a bill that I introduced as part of my ongoing interest over the state of our nation's cybersecurity. This bill takes concrete steps to help strengthen federal government cybersecurity. The most important steps are encouraging federal agencies to adopt the National Institute of Standards and Technology's (NIST) Cybersecurity Framework, which is used by many private businesses, and directing NIST to initiate individual cybersecurity audits of priority federal agencies to determine the extent to which each agency is meeting the information security standards developed by the Institute. NIST's in-house experts develop government-wide technical standards and guidelines under the Federal Information Security Modernization Act of 2014. And NIST experts also developed, through collaborations between government and private sector, the Framework for Improving Critical Infrastructure Cybersecurity that federal agencies are now required to use pursuant to the President's recent Cybersecurity Executive Order. I was very pleased to read that language.

Considering the growing attempts to infiltrate information systems, there is an urgent need to assure Americans that all federal agencies are doing everything that they can to protect government networks and sensitive data. The status quo simply is not working. We can't put up with more bureaucratic excuses and delays.

NIST's cyber expertise is a singular asset. We should take full advantage of that asset, starting with the very important step of annual NIST cyber audits of high priority federal agencies.

As cyber-attacks and cyber criminals continue to evolve and become more sophisticated, our government's cyber defenses must also adapt in order to protect vital public services and shield hundreds of millions of Americans' confidential information.

We will hear from our witnesses today about lessons learned from the WannaCry attack and how the government can bolster the security of its systems. We must keep in mind that the next cyber-attack is just around the corner, and it could have a far greater impact than what we have seen thus far. Our federal government—our government systems need to be better protected, and that starts with more accountability, responsibility, and transparency by federal agencies.

Thank you, and I look forward to hearing our panel.

[The prepared statement of Mr. Abraham follows:]

<table>
<tr><td>For Immediate Release
June 15, 2017</td><td>Media Contact: Kristina Baum
(202) 225-6371</td></tr>
</table>

Statement of Vice Chairman Ralph Abraham (R-La.)
Bolstering the Government's Cybersecurity: Lessons Learned from WannaCry

Vice Chairman Abraham: Thank you Mr. Chairman.

Over the last few years, we have seen an alarming increase in the number and intensity of cyber-attacks. These attacks by cyber criminals and by unfriendly governments have compromised the personal information of millions of Americans, jeopardized thousands of our businesses and their employees, and threatened interruption of critical public services. The recent WannaCry ransomware attack demonstrates that cyber-attacks are continuing to go from bad to worse.

This most recent large-scale cyber attack affected more than one to two million systems in more than 190 countries. Nevertheless, it appears that the impact could have been much more catastrophic considering how fast this ransomware spread.

While organizations and individuals within the United States were largely unscathed, due in part to a security researcher identifying a web-based "kill switch," the potential destructiveness of WannaCry warns us to expect similar attacks in the future. Before those attacks happen, we need to make sure that our information systems are ready.

During a Research and Technology Subcommittee hearing earlier this year, a witness representing the U.S. Government Accountability Office (GAO) testified that, "Over the past several years, GAO has made about 2,500 recommendations to federal agencies to enhance their information security programs and controls. As of February 2017, about 1,000 recommendations had not been implemented."

It is clear that the status quo in federal government cyber security is a virtual invitation for more cyber-attacks. We must take strong steps in order to properly secure our systems and databases before another cyber-attack like WannaCry literally puts our government up for ransom.

On March 1, 2017, this Committee approved H.R. 1224, the NIST Cybersecurity Framework, Assessment, and Auditing Act of 2017, a bill that I introduced as part of my ongoing interest over the state of our nation's cybersecurity.

This bill takes concrete steps to help strengthen Federal government cybersecurity. The most important steps are encouraging federal agencies to adopt the National Institute of Standards and Technology's (NIST) Cybersecurity Framework, which is used by many private businesses, and directing NIST to initiate individual cybersecurity audits of priority Federal agencies to determine the extent to which each agency is meeting the information security standards developed by the Institute.

NIST's in-house experts develop government-wide technical standards and guidelines under the Federal Information Security Modernization Act of 2014. And NIST experts also developed, through collaborations between government and private sector, the Framework for Improving Critical Infrastructure Cybersecurity that federal agencies are now required to use pursuant to the President's recent Cybersecurity Executive Order. I was very pleased to read that language.

Considering the growing attempts to infiltrate information systems, there is an urgent need to assure Americans that all federal agencies are doing everything that they can to protect government networks and sensitive data. The status quo simply isn't working. We can't put up with more bureaucratic excuses and delays.

NIST's cyber expertise is a singular asset. We should take full advantage of that asset, starting with the very important step of annual NIST cyber audits of high priority federal agencies.

As cyber-attacks and cyber criminals continue to evolve and become more sophisticated, our government's cyber defenses must adapt, too, in order to protect vital public services and shield hundreds of millions of Americans' confidential information.

We will hear from our witnesses today about lessons learned from the WannaCry attack and how the government can bolster the security of its systems. We must keep in mind that the next cyber attack is just around the corner, and it could have a far greater impact than what we have seen thus far.

Our government systems need to be better protected, and that starts with more accountability, responsibility, and transparency by federal agencies.

Thank you and I look forward to hearing from our panel.

###

Chairman LaHood. Thank you, Mr. Abraham.

I now recognize the Ranking Member of the Research and Technology Subcommittee, my colleague from Illinois, Mr. Lipinski, for an opening statement.

Mr. Lipinski. Thank you, Chairman LaHood, and I want to thank you and Vice Chair Abraham for holding this hearing on cybersecurity and lessons learned from the WannaCry ransomware attack last month.

The good news is that U.S. government information systems were not negatively impacted by the WannaCry attack. This was a clear victory for our cyber defenses. However, I believe there are lessons to be learned from successes as well as failures. A combination of factors likely contributed to this success, including getting rid of most of our outdated Windows operating systems, diligently installing security patches, securing critical IT assets, and maintaining robust network perimeter defenses.

As we know, Microsoft sent out a security patch for this vulnerability in March, two months before the WannaCry attack. These and other factors played a role in minimizing damage to U.S. businesses as well. However, WannaCry and its impact on other countries serves as yet another reminder that we must never be complacent in our cybersecurity defenses. The threats are ever evolving, and our policies must be robust yet flexible enough to allow our defenses to evolve accordingly.

The Federal Information Security Modernization Act, or FISMA, laid out key responsibilities for the security of civilian information systems. Under FISMA, DHS and OMB have central roles in development and implementation of policies as well as in incident tracking and response. NIST develops and updates security standards and guidelines both informing and responsive to the policies established by OMB. Each agency is responsible for its own FISMA compliance, and each Office of Inspector General is required to audit its own agency's compliance with FISMA on an annual basis. We must continue to support agencies in their efforts to be compliant with FISMA while conducting careful oversight.

In 2014, NIST released the Cybersecurity Framework for Critical Infrastructure, which is currently being updated to Framework Version 1.1. While it is still too early to evaluate its full impact, it appears the Framework is being widely used across industry sectors.

Our Committee recently reported out a bipartisan bill, H.R. 2105, that I was pleased to cosponsor, that would ensure that the Cybersecurity Framework is easily usable by our nation's small businesses. I hope we can get it to the President's desk quickly. In the meantime, the President's recent cybersecurity Executive Order directs federal agencies to use the Framework to manage their own cybersecurity risk. As we have heard in prior hearings, many experts have called for this step, and I applaud the Administration for moving ahead.

I join Mr. Beyer in urging the Administration to fill the many vacant positions across our agencies that would be responsible for implementing the Framework as well as shepherding the myriad reports required by the Executive Order.

Finally, I will take this opportunity to express my disappointment in the Administration's budget proposal for NIST. The top-line budget cut of 25 percent was so severe that if it were implemented, NIST would have no choice but to reduce its cybersecurity efforts. This represents the epitome of penny-wise, pound-foolish decision making. NIST is among the best of the best when it comes to cybersecurity research and standards, and our modest taxpayer investment in their efforts helps secure the information systems not just of our federal government, but our entire economy. I trust that my colleagues will join me in ensuring that NIST receives robust funding in the fiscal year 2018 budget and doesn't suffer the drastic cut requested by the President.

Thank you to the expert witnesses for being here this morning, and I look forward to your testimony. I yield back.

[The prepared statement of Mr. Lipinski follows:]

<u>OPENING STATEMENT</u>
Ranking Member Dan Lipinski (D-IL)
of the Subcommittee on Research and Technology

Committee on Science, Space & Technology
Subcommittee on Oversight
Subcommittee on Research & Technology
"Bolstering the Government's Cybersecurity: Lessons Learned from WannaCry"
June 15, 2017

Thank you Chairman LaHood and Chairwoman Comstock for holding this hearing on cybersecurity and lessons learned from the WannaCry ransomware attack last month.

The good news is that U.S. government information systems were not harmed by the WannaCry attack. This was a clear victory for our cyberdefenses. However, I believe there are lessons to be learned from successes as well as failures. A combination of factors likely contributed to this success, including getting rid of most of our outdated Windows operating systems, diligently installing security patches, securing critical IT assets, and maintaining robust network perimeter defenses. As we know, Microsoft sent out a security patch for this vulnerability in March, two months before the WannaCry attack. These and other factors played a role in minimizing damage to U.S. businesses as well.

However, WannaCry and its impact on other countries serves as yet another reminder that we must never be complacent in our cybersecurity defenses. The threats are ever evolving, and our policies must be robust yet flexible enough to allow our defenses to evolve accordingly.

The Federal Information Security Modernization Act, or FISMA, laid out key responsibilities for the security of civilian information systems. Under FISMA, DHS and OMB have central roles in development and implementation of policies as well as in incident tracking and response. NIST develops and updates security standards and guidelines both informing and responsive to the policies established by OMB. Each agency is responsible for its own FISMA compliance, and each Office of Inspector General is required to audit its own agency's compliance with FISMA on an annual basis. We must continue to support agencies in their efforts to be compliant with FISMA while conducting careful oversight.

In 2014, NIST released the Cybersecurity Framework for Critical Infrastructure, which is currently being updated to Framework Version 1.1. While it is still too early to evaluate its full impact, it appears the Framework is being widely used across industry sectors. Our Committee recently reported out a bipartisan bill, H.R. 2105, that I was pleased to cosponsor, that would ensure that the Cybersecurity Framework is easily usable by our nation's small businesses. I hope we can get it to the President's desk quickly. In the meantime, the President's recent cybersecurity Executive Order directs Federal agencies to use the Framework to manage their own cybersecurity risk. As we have heard in prior hearings, many experts have called for this step, and I applaud the Administration for moving ahead. I join Mr. Beyer in urging the

Administration to fill the many vacant positions across our agencies that would be responsible for implementing the Framework as well as shepherding the myriad reports required by the Executive Order.

Finally, I will take this opportunity to express my disappointment in the Administration's budget proposal for NIST. The top-line budget cut of 25 percent was so severe that if it were implemented, NIST would have no choice but to reduce its cybersecurity efforts. This represents the epitome of penny-wise, pound-foolish decision making. NIST is among the best of the best when it comes to cybersecurity research and standards, and our modest taxpayer investment in their efforts helps secure the information systems not just of our federal government, but our entire economy. I trust that my colleagues will join me in ensuring that NIST receives robust funding in the FY18 budget and doesn't suffer the drastic cut requested by the President.

Thank you to the expert witnesses for being here this morning. I look forward to your testimony. I yield back.

Chairman LaHood. Thank you, Mr. Lipinski.

At this time I now recognize the Chairman of the full Committee, Mr. Smith.

Chairman Smith. Thank you, Mr. Chairman. I appreciate your holding this hearing as well as the Research and Technology Subcommittee Vice Chairman sitting next to me, Ralph Abraham, for holding the hearing as well.

In the wake of last month's WannaCry ransomware attack, today's hearing is a necessary part of an important conversation the federal government must have as we look for ways to improve our federal cybersecurity posture. While WannaCry failed to compromise federal government systems, it is almost certain that outcome was due in part to a measure of chance.

Rather than seeing this outcome as a sign of bulletproof cybersecurity defenses, we must instead increase our vigilance to better identify constantly evolving cybersecurity threats. This is particularly true since many cyber experts predict that we will experience an attack similar to WannaCry that is more sophisticated in nature, carrying with it an even greater possibility of widespread disruption and destruction. Congress should not allow cybersecurity to be ignored across government agencies.

I am proud of the work the Committee has accomplished to improve the federal government's cybersecurity posture. During the last Congress, the Committee conducted investigations into the Federal Deposit Insurance Corporation, the Internal Revenue Service, and the Office of Personnel Management, as well as passed key legislation aimed at providing the government with the tools it needs to strengthen its cybersecurity posture.

President Trump understands the importance of bolstering our cybersecurity. He signed a recent Executive Order on cybersecurity, which is a vital step towards ensuring the federal government is positioned to detect, deter, and defend against emerging threats.

Included in the President's Executive Order is a provision mandating that Executive Branch departments and agencies implement NIST's Cybersecurity Framework. While continuously updating its Cybersecurity Framework, NIST takes into account innovative cybersecurity measures from its private-sector partners. NIST's collaborative efforts help to ensure that those entities that follow the Framework are aware of the most pertinent, effective, and cutting-edge cybersecurity measures. I strongly believe the President's decision to make NIST's Framework mandatory for the federal government will serve to strengthen the government's ability to defend its systems against advanced cyber threats like with the recent WannaCry ransomware attack.

Similarly, the Committee's NIST Cybersecurity Framework, Assessment, and Auditing Act of 2017, sponsored by Representative Abraham, draws on findings from the Committee's numerous hearings and investigations related to cybersecurity, which underscore the immediate need for a rigorous approach to protecting U.S. cybersecurity infrastructure and capabilities.

Like the President's recent Executive Order, this legislation promotes federal use of the NIST Cybersecurity Framework by providing guidance that agencies may use to incorporate the Framework into risk mitigation efforts. Additionally, the bill directs NIST to establish a working group with the responsibility of developing key metrics for federal agencies to use.

I hope that our discussions here today will highlight distinct areas where cybersecurity improvement is necessary, while offering recommendations to ensure cybersecurity objectives stay at the forefront of our national security policy discussions.

And with that, I'll yield back, Mr. Chairman.

[The prepared statement of Chairman Smith follows:]

COMMITTEE ON
SCIENCE, SPACE, & TECHNOLOGY
Lamar Smith, Chairman

For Immediate Release
June 15, 2017

Media Contact: Kristina Baum
(202) 225-6371

Statement of Chairman Lamar Smith (R-Texas)
Bolstering the Government's Cybersecurity: Lessons Learned from WannaCry

Chairman Smith: I would like to thank Oversight Subcommittee Chairman LaHood and Research and Technology Subcommittee Vice Chairman Abraham for holding today's hearing.

In the wake of last month's WannaCry ransomware attack, today's hearing is a necessary part of an important conversation the federal government must have as we look for ways to improve our federal cybersecurity posture. While WannaCry failed to compromise federal government systems, it is almost certain that outcome was due in part to a measure of chance.

Rather than seeing this outcome as a sign of bulletproof cybersecurity defenses, we must instead increase our vigilance to better identify constantly evolving cybersecurity threats. This is particularly true since many cyber experts predict that we will experience an attack similar to WannaCry that is more sophisticated in nature, carrying with it an even greater possibility of widespread disruption and destruction. Congress should not allow cybersecurity to be ignored across government agencies.

I am proud of the work the Committee has accomplished to improve the federal government's cybersecurity posture.

During the last congress, the Committee conducted investigations into the Federal Deposit Insurance Corporation, the Internal Revenue Service, and the Office of Personnel Management, as well as passed key legislation aimed at providing the government with the tools it needs to strengthen its cybersecurity posture.

President Trump understands the importance of bolstering our cybersecurity. He signed a recent Executive Order on cybersecurity, which is a vital step toward ensuring the federal government is positioned to detect, deter, and defend against emerging threats. Included in the President's Executive Order is a provision mandating that Executive Branch departments and agencies implement NIST's Cybersecurity Framework.

While continuously updating its Cybersecurity Framework, NIST takes into account innovative cybersecurity measures from its private sector partners.

NIST's collaborative efforts help to ensure that those entities that follow the Framework are aware of the most pertinent, effective, and cutting edge cybersecurity measures.

I strongly believe the President's decision to make NIST's Framework mandatory for the federal government will serve to strengthen the government's ability to defend its systems against advanced cyber threats like the recent WannaCry ransomware attack.

Similarly, the Committee's NIST Cybersecurity Framework, Assessment, and Auditing Act of 2017, sponsored by Representative Abraham, draws on findings from the Committee's numerous hearings and investigations related to cybersecurity. It underscores the immediate need for a rigorous approach to protecting U.S. cybersecurity infrastructure and capabilities.

Like the President's recent Executive Order, this legislation promotes federal use of the NIST Cybersecurity Framework by providing guidance that agencies may use to incorporate the Framework into risk mitigation efforts. Additionally, the bill directs NIST to establish a working group with the responsibility of developing key metrics for federal agencies to use.

I hope that our discussions here today will highlight distinct areas where cybersecurity improvement is necessary, while offering recommendations to ensure cybersecurity objectives stay at the forefront of our national security policy discussions.

###

Chairman LAHOOD. Thank you, Chairman Smith.

At this time let me introduce our witnesses here today.

Our first witness is Mr. Salim Neino, Founder and Chief Executive Officer of Kryptos Logic. Mr. Neino is credited with discovering new solutions for companies such as IBM, Dell, Microsoft, and Avaya. He received his bachelor's degree in computer science from California State University at Long Beach. A Kryptos Logic employee, as we've discussed, in the U.K. is credited with largely stopping the WannaCry attack. We'll hear more about that during Mr. Neino's testimony today.

Our second witness today is Dr. Charles Romine, Director of the Information Technology Laboratory at NIST. Dr. Romine received both his bachelor's degree in mathematics and his Ph.D. in applied mathematics from the University of Virginia.

Our third witness, Mr. Touhill, is a retired Brigadier General in the United States Air Force. He is currently an Adjunct Professor of Cybersecurity and Risk Management at Carnegie Mellon University. Previously, he was chosen by President Obama to serve as the Nation's Chief Information Security Officer. Mr. Touhill received his bachelor's degree from Penn State University and a master's degree in systems management and information systems from the University of South—I'm sorry—Southern California.

And our final witness today is Dr. Hugh Thompson, Chief Technology Officer for Symantec. Dr. Thompson also serves as an Advisory Board Member for the Anti-Malware Testing Standards Organization and on the Editorial Board of IEEE Security and Privacy magazine. Dr. Thompson received his bachelor's degree and master's degree and Ph.D. in applied mathematics from the Florida Institute of Technology.

We're glad you're all here today and look forward to your valuable testimony. I now recognize Dr. Neino for five minutes to present his testimony.

TESTIMONY OF MR. SALIM NEINO,
CHIEF EXECUTIVE OFFICER,
KRYPTOS LOGIC

Mr. NEINO. Thank you, Chairman. Chairman LaHood, Vice Chairman Abraham, Chairman Smith, Ranking Member Beyer, and Ranking Member Lipinski, thank you for the opportunity to appear before you today at this joint Subcommittee hearing. We greatly appreciate your interest in cybersecurity and look forward to sharing our thoughts and perspectives with you and your members.

On May 12, 2017, Kryptos Logic identified a high-velocity, high-impact global security threat with the immediate potential to cause an immeasurable amount of damage. While the intent of this threat was unclear and its motives and origins ambiguous, it was immediately evident that its approach was unusually reckless. This threat has now popularly become known as "WannaCry." It was at this time that Marcus Hutchins, our Director of Threat Intelligence for Kryptos Logic's Vantage, our breach monitoring platform, notified me of our team's active monitoring of the developing situation. On this date at approximately 10:00 a.m. Eastern time, while investigating the code of WannaCry, we identified what looked like an anti-detection mechanism, which tested for the existence of a certain random-looking domain name. Our team proceeded to register the domain associated to this mechanism and directed it to one of the sinkholes controlled by and hosted on the Kryptos Logic network infrastructure. We then noticed and confirmed that the propagation of the WannaCry attack had come to a standstill because of what we refer to as its kill switch having been activated by our domain registration.

While our efforts effectively stopped the attack, and prevented WannaCry from continuing to deploy its ransom component, we knew that by then the attack had already propagated freely for many hours, at minimum. Based on the velocity of the attack, estimated by sampling data we collected from our infrastructure currently blocking the attack, we believe had that anywhere between 1 to 2 million systems may have been affected in the hours prior to activating the kill switch, contrary to the widely reported and more conservative estimate of 200,000 systems.

One month after registering the kill-switch domain, we have mitigated over 60 million infection attempts. Approximately 7 million of those in the United States, and we estimate that these could have impacted at minimum 10 to 15 million unique systems.

I will note that the largest attack we thwarted and measured to date from WannaCry was not on May 12th or 13th when the attack started, but began suddenly on June 8th and 9th on a well-funded hospital in the east coast of the United States. It is very likely the health system is still unaware of the event. We measured approximately 275,000 thwarted infection attempts within a 2-day period. Another hospital was also hit on May 30th in another part of the country. A high school in the Midwest was just hit at the beginning of June 9th.

Presumably every system at this location would have had its data held hostage if not for Kryptos Logic's kill switch. Moreover, Kryptos Logic has been under constant attack by unidentified attackers attempting to knock our systems offline, thus disabling the kill switch and further propagating the attack. The earlier of these attacks came by the well-known Mirai botnet which took down large portions of the United Kingdom, Germany and parts of the East Coast of the United States earlier this year. Despite these attempts, our systems remained resilient and we increased counter-intelligence measures to mitigate the amplitude of the attacks against us.

We believe the success of WannaCry illustrates two key facts about our nation's systems: Vulnerabilities exist at virtually every level of our computer infrastructure, ranging from operating systems to browsers, from media players to Internet routers. Exploiting and weaponizing such vulnerabilities has a surprisingly low entry barrier: anyone can join in, including rogue teenagers, nation states, and everyone in between.

So, how do we adapt and overcome/mitigate these weaknesses? While many cybersecurity experts who have come before me offer the usual gloomy "there are no silver bullets," I've had the opportunity to play on both fronts: on offense, via penetration testing and red team competitions, and on defense, providing protection to Global 100 organizations with very high enterprise risks. Our attack responses must be more agile and with higher velocity and intensity.

While the nation has considerable literature on risk, maturity models and various frameworks, the actual resources for cyber defense are scarce as there simply is not presently an adequate level of highly skilled, highly experienced, and highly available operators in the cybersecurity field. While there is no shortage of good ideas which claim to be able to solve an infinite amount of problems, every subsequent idea needs development, support, testing, maintenance, et cetera, all of which we characterize as developer debt.

Unfortunately, many of these solutions take too long to procure and end up being outdated and essentially useless before the ink dries on the paper it is written on. I am optimistic, however, that there is a successful path and strategy forward. Application and software-level mitigations which protect against the exploitation techniques used by hackers have moved the needle to protect against exploitation of the very fabric on which we build our defense assumptions. Mitigations able and incomplete are nonetheless effective and have increased the cost of identifying vulnerabilities in systems and developing programs to exploit them. Other mitigations include various design approaches like compartmentalization of data, systems and transmissions. Such mitigations have measurably raised the bar required for mass exploitation in critical communications software like Internet browsers, web servers, and other protocols which are fundamental to business continuity.

Investing in technology doesn't necessarily guarantee any actual improvement. In fact, one could argue that introducing more technology stack exacerbates the maintenance debt and creates immediate monetary loss because there are few metrics or analytics to actually measure the effectiveness of any particular technology. This is because we are typically years behind the attack in terms of the sword and shield battle.

As these resources ebb and flow, knowledge gaps are created and the loss of a domain knowledge specialists who cannot immediately fill these gaps and replace them.

We also must be less risk averse in terms of the defensive operations we undertake, more open to failure, and ready to adapt and learn from these failures. We need a stronger focus on threat modeling and fire-drill simulations that will be focused on the events of a magnitude which would cause significant damage. A significant response with the WannaCry incident was that there was no real guidance or course of action that was well communicated. The media focused on the points contrary to defense—whodunit?—and this incident could have resulted in a complete breakdown of processes had this been an unpatched zero-day vulnerability and there was no luxury of a kill switch.

The largest success, though incomplete, was the ability for the FBI and the NCSC of the United Kingdom to aggregate and disseminate the information Kryptos Logic provided so that affected organizations could respond. Information sharing can be valuable but our framework can be vastly improved by triaging cybersecurity threats and events of magnitude in a clear and repeatable scale, not too dissimilar to the Richter scale, which measures the energy released in an earthquake. Likewise, a scale that takes the technical and social elements of a threat into account to evaluate its destructive power enables first responders—us—to better organize and mobilize focus on the most important areas of risk.

While there do exist various scoring systems for evaluating the purely technical element of a threat, they fall short in terms of clear and actionable information outside of information technology. We focus too much on application-specific vulnerabilities with abstruse names like MS17–010, and none of these values are effective in quantifying the overall impact potential of a wider global environment. We need an easier-to-grasp method of prioritizing threats that have a large-scale destructive potential in context, like WannaCry.

To this end, once we have determined a method to evaluate the risks with respect to the aforementioned technical and contextual specifics, we can do—we can apply the appropriate mitigations.

In conclusion, one of the largest issues is the transitory nature of a crisis. This message still has not resonated of the destructive potential of these attacks and the importance of its awareness. We think this can be explained simply by the fact organizations are too slow to adapt to such a volatile landscape, there is a vast human resource shortage, and little by way of metrics to demonstrate return on investment in defensive technologies.

Again, I thank the Subcommittee for inviting me to appear today to discuss Kryptos Logic's involvement in lessons learned for WannaCry, and I welcome the opportunity to answer any questions you may have when they're fielded.

[The prepared statement of Mr. Neino follows:]

Prepared Testimony of Salim Neino, Chief Executive Officer, Kryptos Logic

U.S. House of Representatives Committee on Science, Space & Technology, Joint Subcommittee on Oversight and Subcommittee on Research and Technology Hearing

15 June 2017

Chairman LaHood, Chairwoman Comstock, Ranking Member Beyer and Ranking Member Lipinski, thank you for the opportunity to appear before you today at this joint Subcommittee hearing. We greatly appreciate your interest in cybersecurity and look forward to sharing our thoughts and perspectives with you and your Members.

<u>WannaCry Involvement and Response</u>

On May 12th, 2017, Kryptos Logic identified a high-velocity, high-impact global security threat with the immediate potential to cause an immeasurable amount of damage. While the intent of this threat was unclear and its motives and origins ambiguous, it was immediately evident that its approach was unusually reckless. This threat has now popularly become known as ``WannaCry.'' It was at this time that Marcus Hutchins, Director of Threat Intelligence for Kryptos Logic's Vantage (our breach monitoring platform and feed) notified me of our team's active monitoring of the developing situation.

On this date at approximately 10:00 a.m. Eastern time, while investigating the code of WannaCry, we identified what looked like an anti-detection mechanism, which tested for the existence of a certain random-looking domain name. Our team proceeded to register the domain associated to this mechanism and directed it to one of the "sinkholes" controlled by and hosted on the Kryptos Logic network infrastructure. We then noticed and confirmed that the propagation of the WannaCry attack had come to a standstill because of what we refer to as its ``kill-switch'' having been activated by our domain registration.

While our efforts effectively stopped the attack, and prevented WannaCry from continuing to deploy its ransom component (which irreversibly destroys important files) we knew that by then the attack had already propagated freely for hours, at minimum. Based on the velocity of the attack, estimated by sampling data we collected from our infrastructure currently blocking the attack, we believe had that anywhere between 1-2 million systems may have been affected in the hours prior to activating the kill-switch, contrary to the widely reported – and more conservative – estimate of 200,000 systems.

One month after registering the kill-switch domain, we have mitigated over 60 million infection attempts – approximately 7 million in the United States – and we estimate that these could have impacted a minimum 10-15 million unique systems. I will note that the largest attack we thwarted and measured to date from WannaCry was not on May 12 or 13th when the attack started, but began suddenly on June 8th and 9th on a well-funded hospital in the east coast of the United States. It is very likely the health system is still unaware of the event. We measured approximately 275,000 thwarted infection attempts within a 2-day period. Another hospital was hit on May 30th, in another part of the country. A high-school in the Midwest was just hit beginning on June 9th.

Presumably every system at this location would have had its data held hostage if not for Kryptos Logic's kill-switch.

Moreover, Kryptos Logic has been under constant attack by unidentified attackers attempting to knock our systems offline, thus disabling the kill-switch and further propagating the attack. The earlier of these attacks came by the well-known Mirai botnet which took down large portions of the United Kingdom, Germany and part of the east coast of the United States earlier this year. Despite these attempts, our systems remained resilient and we increased counter-intelligence measures to mitigate the amplitude of the attacks against us.

Observations and Thoughts Regarding Cybersecurity Response and Policy

We believe the success of WannaCry illustrates two key facts about our nation's systems:

- Vulnerabilities exist at virtually every level of our computer infrastructure, ranging from operating systems to browsers, from media players to Internet routers;

- Exploiting and weaponizing such vulnerabilities has a surprisingly low entry barrier: anyone can join in, including rogue teenagers, nation states, and everyone in-between.

So, how do we adapt and overcome/mitigate these weaknesses? While many cybersecurity experts who have come before me offer the usual gloomy "there are no silver bullets," I have had the opportunity to play on both fronts; on offense, via penetration testing and competitive hacking (including winning Defcon CTF, a kinetic and defense based hacking tournament) and on defense, providing protection to Global 100 organizations with very high enterprise risks.

Our attack responses must be more agile and with higher velocity and intensity. While the nation has considerable literature on risk, maturity models and various frameworks, the actual resources for cyberdefense (execution) are scarce as there simply is not presently an adequate level of highly skilled, highly experienced, and highly available operators in the cybersecurity field. While there is no shortage of "ideas" which claim to be able to solve an infinite amount of problems, each and every subsequent idea needs development, support, testing, maintenance, etc. -- all of which we characterize as "developer debt." Unfortunately, many of these solutions take too long to procure and end up being outdated - and essentially useless - before the ink dries on the paper it is written on.

I am optimistic, however, that there is a successful path and strategy forward. Application and software level mitigations which protect against the exploitation techniques used by hackers have moved the needle to protect against exploitation of the very fabric on which we build our defense assumptions. Mitigations, albeit incomplete, are nonetheless effective, and have increased the cost of identifying vulnerabilities in systems and developing programs to exploit them. Other mitigations include various design approaches like compartmentalization of data, systems, and transmissions. Such mitigations have measurably raised the bar required for mass exploitation in critical communications software like Internet browsers, web servers, and other protocols which are fundamental to business continuity.

<u>As assessing risk is the bane of security, what actually is effective?</u>

Investing in technology doesn't necessarily guarantee any actual improvement; in fact, one could argue that introducing more technology stack exacerbates maintenance debt and creates immediate monetary loss because there are few metrics or analytics to actually measure the effectiveness of any particular technology. This is because we are typically years behind attackers in terms of the "sword/shield battle." As these resources ebb and flow, "knowledge gaps" are created, e.g., the loss of a domain knowledge specialist who cannot be immediately replaced.

We also must be less risk averse in terms of the defensive operations we undertake, more open to failure and ready to adapt and learn from these failures. We need a stronger focus on threat modeling and "fire drill" simulations that will be focused on the events of a magnitude which could cause significant damage. A significant response failure with the WannaCry incident was that there was no real guidance or course of action that was well communicated; the media focused on the points contrary to defense (who did it?), and this incident could have resulted in a complete breakdown of processes had this been an unpatched "zero-day" vulnerability and there was no luxury of a "kill-switch".

The largest success, though incomplete, was the ability for the FBI and NCSC of the United Kingdom to aggregate and disseminate the information Kryptos Logic provided so that affected organizations could respond. Information sharing can be valuable but our framework can be vastly improved by triaging cybersecurity threats and events of magnitude in a clear and repeatable scale, not dissimilar to the Richter scale, which measures the energy released in an earthquake. Likewise, a scale that takes the technical and social elements of a threat into account to evaluate its destructive power enables first responders – us – to better organize and mobilize focus on the most important areas of risk.

While there do exist various scoring systems for evaluating the purely technical element of a threat, they fall short in terms of clear and actionable information outside of information technology. We focus too much on application specific vulnerabilities with abstruse names like MS17-010, and none of these values are effective in quantifying the overall impact potential on a wider global environment. We need an easier to grasp method of prioritizing threats that have a large scale destructive potential in context, like WannaCry. To this end, once we have determined a method to evaluate attacks with respect to the aforementioned technical and contextual specifics, we may then place efforts on the simulation of these high-risk cases against our networks and further develop better communication methods, courses of action, and of course preempt these attacks with improved resiliency given the new awareness of these risks and their appropriate mitigations.

In conclusion, one of the largest issues is the transitory nature of a crisis. The message still has not resonated of the destructive potential of these attacks and the importance of its awareness. We think this can be explained simply by the fact their organizations are too slow to adapt to such a volatile landscape, there is a vast human resource shortage, and little by way of metrics to demonstrate return on investment in defensive technologies.

Again, I thank the Subcommittee for inviting me to appear before you today to discuss Kryptos Logic's involvement in lessons learned for WannaCry, and I welcome the opportunity to answer any questions you may have.

KRYPTOS LOGIC

Salim Neino, Chief Executive Officer, Kryptos Logic

Salim Neino is the Founder and CEO of Kryptos Logic, a Cyber Security company based in Los Angeles, California since 2008. Mr. Neino is an information security specialist with emphasis in vulnerability and exploitation research, software mitigation, threat intelligence, and cyber program management. Mr. Neino has been involved in numerous facets of cyber security, including: leading red teams for penetration testing, creating defensive programs and threat intelligence platforms for Global 100 organizations and creating attack and defense frameworks for threat-intelligence. He is credited discovering new mitigations and resolving vulnerabilities for security vendors such as IBM, Dell, Microsoft and Avaya.

Mr. Neino holds a black badge for his team's first place the Defcon 19 CTF hacking competition and has regularly competed in hacking competitions since 2009. Mr. Neino has been a key monthly presenter for threat intelligence briefings to the critical infrastructure community through the Water Information Sharing and Analysis Center (Water-ISAC) and gives regular briefings on the state of infrastructure security, threats, and defensive solutions to protect systems from targeted attacks.

Mr. Neino formed Kryptos Logic by assimilating recognized strategic computer security experts for the purpose of developing scalable solutions utilizing data-driven intelligence and Big data analysis capabilities. Specifically, engineering and architecture solutions which could attack or defend at scale and process trillions of security related records per day.

The company's offerings have been galvanized by years of network security experience in numerous industries including academic, government, and commercial. Through Mr. Neino's leadership, Kryptos Logic has developed widely-used security products, threat intelligence platforms, mitigated vulnerabilities, and delivers a secure an approach which enhances security posture for organizations of all sizes.

In May 2017, a solution Kryptos Logic provides - commercially known as Vantage - and its researchers, are credited for bringing down the largest known ransomware cyber-attack in history, referred to as WannaCry or WannaCrypt and Kryptos Logic has since thwarted tens of millions of related ransom attempts.

Chairman LAHOOD. Thank you, Mr. Neino.

I now recognize Dr. Romine for five minutes to present his testimony.

TESTIMONY OF DR. CHARLES H. ROMINE, DIRECTOR, INFORMATION TECHNOLOGY LABORATORY, NATIONAL INSTITUTE OF STANDARDS AND TECHNOLOGY

Dr. ROMINE. Chairmen LaHood and Abraham, Chairman Smith, Ranking Members Beyer and Lipinski, and members of the Subcommittees, thank you for the opportunity to appear before you today to discuss NIST's key roles in cybersecurity and how they relate to recent incidents.

In the area of cybersecurity, NIST has worked with federal agencies, industry and academic since 1972 starting with the development of the Data Encryption Standard when the potential commercial benefit of this technology became clear.

NIST's role to research, develop, and deploy information security standards and technology to protect the federal government's information systems against threats to the confidentiality, integrity, and availability of information and services was recently reaffirmed in the Federal Information Security Modernization Act of 2014.

NIST provides resources to assist organizations in preventing or, at least, quickly recovering from ransomware attacks with trust that the recovered data are accurate, complete, and free of malware, and that the recovered system is trustworthy and capable. NIST's Guide for Cybersecurity Event Recovery provides guidance to help organizations plan and prepare for recovery from a cyber event and integrate the processes and procedures into their enterprise risk management plans. The Guide discusses hypothetical cyber-attack scenarios including one focused on ransomware and steps taken to recover from the attack.

Three years ago, NIST issued the Framework for Improving Critical Infrastructure Cybersecurity, or the Framework. The Framework created through tight collaboration between industry and government consists of voluntary standards, guidelines and practices to promote the protection of critical infrastructure.

In the case of WannaCry and similar ransomware, the Framework prompts decisions affecting infection by the ransomware, propagation of the ransomware, and recovery from it. While the Framework does not prescribe a baseline of cybersecurity for organizations, for instance, a baseline that would have prevented WannaCry, it does prompt a sequence of interrelated cybersecurity risk management decisions, which should help prevent virus infection and propagation and support expeditious response and recovery activities.

On May 11th, President Trump signed Executive Order 13800, strengthening the cybersecurity of federal networks and critical infrastructure that mandated federal agencies to use the Framework. Under the Executive Order, every federal agency or department will need to manage their cybersecurity risk by using the framework and provide a risk management report to the Director of the Office of Management and Budget and to the Secretary of Homeland Security.

On May 12th, NIST released a draft interagency report, the Cybersecurity Framework Implementation Guidance for Federal Agencies, which provides guidance on how the Framework can be used in the United States Federal Government in conjunction with the current and planned suite of NIST security and privacy risk management standards, guidelines and practices developed in response to the Federal Information Security Management Act, as amended, or FISMA.

Another NIST resource that can assist system administrators in protecting against similar future attacks is the most recent release of the NIST National Software Reference Library, or NSRL. The NSRL provides a collection of software from various sources and unique file profiles, which is most often used by law enforcement, government, and industry organizations to review files on a computer by matching the profiles in the system.

NIST maintains a repository of all known and publicly reported IT vulnerabilities such as the one exploited by the WannaCry malware. The repository, called the National Vulnerability Database, or NVD, is an authoritative source of standardized information on security vulnerabilities that NIST updates dozens of times daily. NIST analyzes and provides a common severity metric to each identified security vulnerability.

NIST recently initiated a project at our National Cybersecurity Center of Excellence, or NCCOE, on data integrity specifically focused on recovering from cyber-attacks. Organizations will be able to use the results of the NCCOE research to recover trusted backups, roll back data to a known good state, alert administrators when there is a change to a critical system, and restore services quickly after a WannaCry-like cyber-attack.

NIST is extremely proud of its role in establishing and improving the comprehensive set of cybersecurity technical solutions, standards, and guidelines to address cyber threats in general and ransomware in particular.

Thank you for the opportunity to testify today on NIST's work in cybersecurity and in preventing ransomware attacks. I'd be happy to answer any questions that you may have.

[The prepared statement of Dr. Romine follows:]

Testimony of

Charles H. Romine, Ph.D.

Director
Information Technology Laboratory
National Institute of Standards and Technology
United States Department of Commerce

Before the
United States House of Representatives
Committee on Science, Space, and Technology
Subcommittee on Oversight and
Subcommittee on Research and Technology

"Bolstering Government Cybersecurity Lessons Learned from WannaCry"

June 15, 2017

Introduction

Chairman LaHood, Chairwoman Comstock, Ranking Member Beyer, and Ranking Member Lipinski, and members of the Subcommittees, I am Dr. Charles Romine, the Director of the Information Technology Laboratory (ITL) at the Department of Commerce's National Institute of Standards and Technology (NIST). Thank you for the opportunity to appear before you today to discuss NIST's key roles in cybersecurity. Specifically, today I will discuss NIST's activities that help strengthen the Nation's cybersecurity capabilities.

The Role of NIST in Cybersecurity

With programs focused on national priorities from advanced manufacturing and the digital economy to precision metrology, quantum science, biosciences, and more, NIST's overall mission is to promote U.S. innovation and industrial competitiveness by advancing measurement science, standards, and technology in ways that enhance economic security and improve our quality of life.

In the area of cybersecurity, NIST has worked with federal agencies, industry, and academia since 1972, starting with the development of the Data Encryption Standard, when the potential commercial benefit of this technology became clear. NIST's role, to research, develop and deploy information security standards and technology to protect the Federal Government's information systems against threats to the confidentiality, integrity, and availability of information and services, was strengthened through the Computer Security Act of 1987 (Public Law 100-235), broadened through the Federal Information Security Management Act of 2002 (FISMA; 44 U.S.C. § 3541[1]) and reaffirmed in the Federal Information Security Modernization Act of 2014 (Public Law 113-283). In addition, the Cybersecurity Enhancement Act of 2014 (Public Law 113-274) authorizes NIST to facilitate and support the development of voluntary, industry-led cybersecurity standards and best practices for critical infrastructure.

NIST standards and guidelines are developed in an open, transparent, and collaborative manner that enlists broad expertise from around the world. While developed for federal agency use, these resources are often voluntarily adopted by other organizations, including small and medium-sized businesses, educational institutions, and state, local, and tribal governments, because NIST's standards and guidelines are effective and accepted globally. NIST disseminates its resources through a variety of means that encourage the broad sharing of information security standards, guidelines, and practices, including outreach to stakeholders, participation in government and industry events, and online mechanisms.

---

[1] FISMA was enacted as Title III of the E-Government Act of 2002 (Public Law 107-347; 116 Stat. 2899).

Recent Malware Attack

Since May 12, a cyberattack impacted more than 230,000 computers in over 150 countries, including the United Kingdom, Russia, and India. Major health systems, telecommunications providers, and railway companies across Europe felt the impact of the attack.

The cause of the attack is reported to be a ransomware called WannaCry. This type of malicious software blocks access to systems and data until a ransom is paid. In this case, the ransomware targets computers running Microsoft Windows operating system by exploiting a vulnerability specific to this system.

WannaCry has spread across local networks and the Internet automatically and has infected systems that have not been secured with recent software updates or are using an older and unsupported operating system. Most of the systems that were infected by the ransomware were running these unsupported operating systems. On March 14, Microsoft had issued a patch to remove the underlying vulnerability for its supported systems. Later, Microsoft also took the unusual step of providing security updates for those unsupported systems, as well.[2]

NIST provides resources to assist organizations in preventing or, at least, quickly recovering from ransomware attacks with trust that the recovered data is accurate, complete, and free of malware and that the recovered system is trustworthy and capable.

To address the issue of cybersecurity in general, and malware in particular, NIST has long worked effectively with industry and federal agencies to help protect the confidentiality, integrity, and availability of information systems. Some of our most significant efforts are addressed below.

Resources to Help Address Malware Incidents

NIST provides standards, best practices, tools, reference implementations, and other resources to help organizations protect assets and detect, respond to, and recover from incidents to minimize the impact of an incident to an organization's mission. The WannaCry incident was new and disruptive, and NIST intends to review the event and its aftermath to ensure that our resources sufficiently address these types of events. Based on our initial review, we believe that many of our past recommendations are applicable to these events, most notably recommendations that can be found in the NIST *Guide for Cybersecurity Event Recovery* and the *Framework for Improving Critical Infrastructure Cybersecurity*, among others.

---

[2] https://blogs.technet.microsoft.com/msrc/2017/05/12/customer-guidance-for-wannacrypt-attacks/

Cybersecurity Event Recovery
Effective planning is a critical component of an organization's preparedness for cyber event recovery. As part of an organization's ongoing information security program, recovery planning enables participants to understand system dependencies; critical roles such as crisis management and incident management; arrangements for alternate communication channels, services, and facilities; and many other elements of business continuity. NIST's *Guide for Cybersecurity Event Recovery* (NIST Special Publication 800-184) provides guidance to help organizations plan and prepare recovery from a cyber-event and integrate the processes and procedures into their enterprise risk management plan.[3] The guide discusses hypothetical cyber-attack scenarios, including a scenario focused on ransomware, and the steps taken to recover from the attack. It provides a detailed description of the pre-conditions required for effective recovery, the activities of the recovery team in the tactical recovery phase, and, after the cyber-attack has been eradicated, the activities performed during the strategic recovery phase.

NIST's *Guide for Cybersecurity Event Recovery* assists organizations in developing an actionable set of steps, or a playbook, the organization can follow to successfully recover from a cyber-event. A playbook can focus on a unique type of cyber-event and can be organization-specific, tailored to fit the dependencies of its people, processes, and technologies. If an active cyber-event is discovered, organizations that do not have in-house expertise to execute a playbook can seek assistance from a trustworthy external party with experience in incident response and recovery, such as the Department of Homeland Security (DHS), an Information Sharing and Analysis Organization (ISAO), or a reputable commercially managed security services provider.

Cybersecurity Framework
Three years ago, NIST issued the *Framework for Improving Critical Infrastructure Cybersecurity* (the Framework) in accordance with Section 7 of Executive Order 13636, "Improving Critical Infrastructure Cybersecurity." The Framework, created through collaboration between industry and government, consists of voluntary standards, guidelines, and practices to promote the protection of critical infrastructure. The voluntary, risk-based prioritized, flexible, repeatable, and cost-effective approach of the Framework helps owners and operators of critical infrastructure to manage cybersecurity-related risk. Although the Framework was originally designed to help protect critical infrastructure, numerous business of all sizes and from many economic sectors use the Framework to manage their cybersecurity risks.

Since the release of the Framework, NIST has strengthened its collaborations with critical infrastructure owners and operators, industry leaders, government partners, and other stakeholders to raise awareness about the Framework, encourage use by organizations across and supporting the critical infrastructure, and develop implementation guides and resources.

The Framework is a valuable tool to help organizations understand and manage cybersecurity risk. It focuses on identifying and protecting key systems and assets and

---

[3] http://nvlpubs.nist.gov/nistpubs/SpecialPublications/NIST.SP.800-184.pdf

on implementing capabilities to detect the occurrence of a cybersecurity event. The Framework also reinforces the importance of capabilities necessary to respond to, and recover from, cybersecurity attacks, including ransomware.

In the case of WannaCry and similar ransomware, the Framework prompts decisions affecting infection by the ransomware, propagation of the ransomware, and recovery from it. For example, the Framework encourages users to understand "data flows"[4] and configure systems minimally to reduce potential vulnerabilities.[5] The Framework identifies network monitoring to "detect potential cybersecurity events,"[6] including the presence of "malicious code,"[7] and to compare them to "expected data flows"[8] in the network to help organizations quickly detect and contain the malicious code and to determine the effectiveness of eradication measures.

WannaCry propagated using a specific operating system vulnerability. The operating system vendor had released a patch nearly two months prior to the first observed instance of WannaCry. The Framework states, "maintenance and repair of organizational assets is performed and logged in a timely manner."[9] Organizations that performed "maintenance and repair" of their operating systems within a two-month window would not have been subject to the spread of WannaCry. Using the Framework, each organization determines its own definition of "timely" to align with its risk tolerance. WannaCry and similar circumstances inform our perspectives on what "timely" means.

An organization's ability to prevent WannaCry from spreading is hinged on identifying systems that are vulnerable and potentially infected and the incident response plans and actions to stop the spread. Recovery is hinged on adequate backups,[10] high-priority system patching,[11] and improvements made to user education and system-patching timelines based on lessons learned.[12]

While the Framework allows an organization to determine its priorities based on its risk tolerance, it also prompts a sequence of interrelated cybersecurity risk management decisions, which should prevent virus infection and propagation and support expeditious response and recovery activities.

On May 11, President Trump signed Executive Order 13800 *Strengthening the Cybersecurity of Federal Networks and Critical Infrastructure* that mandated Federal

---

[4] Identify, Asset Management, Subcategory 3 (ID.AM-3)

[5] Protect, Protective Technology, Subcategory 3 (PR.PT-3)

[6] Detect, Security Continuous Monitoring, Subcategory 1 (DE.CM-1)

[7] Detect, Security Continuous Monitoring, Subcategory 4 (DE.CM-4)

[8] Detect, Anomalies and Events, Subcategory 1 (DE.AE-1)

[9] Protect, Maintenance, Subcategory 1 (PR.MA-1)

[10] Protect, Information Protection Processes and Procedures (PR.IP)

[11] Protect, Maintenance (PR.MA)

[12] Recovery, Improvements (RC.IM)

agencies to use the Framework. Under the Executive Order, every Federal agency or department will need to manage their cybersecurity risk by using the Framework and provide a risk management report to the Director of the Office of Management and Budget and to the Secretary of Homeland Security.[13]

On May 12, NIST released a draft interagency report (NISTIR 8170), *The Cybersecurity Framework: Implementation Guidance for Federal Agencies,* which provides guidance on how the Framework can be used in the U.S. Federal government in conjunction with the current and planned suite of NIST security and privacy risk-management standards, guidelines, and practices developed pursuant to the Federal Information Security Management Act, as amended (FISMA).

This report illustrates eight cases in which Federal agencies can leverage the Framework to address common cybersecurity-related responsibilities. By doing so, agencies can integrate the Framework with key NIST cybersecurity risk-management standards and guidelines already in wide use at various organizational levels.

The goal of these efforts is to allow Federal agencies to build more robust and mature agency-wide cybersecurity risk-management programs. NIST will engage with agencies to add content based on their implementation of the Framework, refine current guidance, and identify additional guidance to provide information that is most helpful to government agencies.

National Software Reference Library
Another NIST resource that can assist system administrators in protecting against similar future attacks is the most recent release of the NIST National Software Reference Library (NSRL). The NSRL provides a collection of software from various sources and unique file profiles (computed from this software), which is most often used by law enforcement, government, and industry organizations to review files on a computer by matching file profiles in the system.

To assist system administrators following the WannaCry attack, the most recent NSRL release includes all Microsoft patches for end-of-life operating system software, such as Windows XP, and the current Windows 10 operating system software, which is a patched version of Windows. NIST is adding a standalone data set to the NSRL, which will include patched versions of supported Windows software that are not Windows 10, such as Windows Server 2016.

National Vulnerability Database
NIST maintains a repository of all known and publicly reported IT vulnerabilities, such as the one exploited by the WannaCry malware. The repository, called the National

---

[13] https://www.whitehouse.gov/the-press-office/2017/05/11/presidential-executive-order-strengthening-cybersecurity-federal

Vulnerability Database (NVD),[14] is an authoritative source of standardized information on security vulnerabilities that NIST updates dozens of times daily. NIST analyzes and provides a common severity metric to each identified security vulnerability.

The NVD is used by security vendors as well as tools and service providers around the world to help them identify whether they have vulnerabilities. For example, the WannaCry malware exploited a vulnerability that was well documented in the NVD database. This vulnerability's impact score, which assesses the severity of a computer system's security vulnerability, ranges between 8.1 and 9.3 (with 10 being the most severe).

Organizations that use the NVD database to identify and address their computer systems' vulnerabilities can better prepare against malware that exploit these vulnerabilities. The patch issued by Microsoft on March 14 was meant to remove such vulnerabilities and allowed computer systems to be protected from the WannaCry malware attack.

Data Integrity
NIST recently initiated a project at our National Cybersecurity Center of Excellence (NCCoE) on data integrity, specifically focused on recovering from cyberattacks. This project will enable organizations to answer questions like what data was corrupted, when was the data corrupted, how was the data corrupted, and who corrupted the data? Organizations will be able to use the results of NCCoE's research to recover trusted backups, rollback data to a known good state, alert administrators when there is a change to a critical system, and restor services quickly after a WannaCry-like cyberattack.

Conclusion

NIST recognizes that it has an essential role to play in helping industry, consumers, and the government to counter cyber-threats, such as those from destructive malware like WannaCry, and enhance the security of the Nation's cyberinfrastructure and capabilities. The outputs from its cybersecurity portfolio allow users to improve their cybersecurity posture, from small and medium businesses to large private and public organizations, including the Federal Government and companies involved with critical infrastructure.

From the NSRL software collection, which includes all Microsoft patches for end-of-life operating system software, to the *Cybersecurity Framework* and the *Guide for Cybersecurity Event Recovery*, which help organizations manage cybersecurity-related risks and prepare for recovery, to the NVD database, which includes all known and publicly reported IT vulnerabilities, NIST provides tools that help various organizations and the Federal Government prepare for future ransomware attacks. By understanding IT vulnerabilities, protecting computer systems against them, and being prepared to

---

[14] https://nvd.nist.gov/vuln/detail/CVE-2017-0145#vulnDescriptionTitle [Link to NVD reference to the main vulnerability exploited by WannaCry]

carry out plans that counter cyberattacks, we can all significantly reduce harms that can result from such attacks.

NIST is extremely proud of its role in establishing and improving the comprehensive set of cybersecurity technical solutions, standards, and guidelines to address cyber-threats, in general, and ransomware, in particular. Thank you for the opportunity to testify today on NIST's work in cybersecurity and in preventing ransomware attacks. I would be happy to answer any questions you may have.

Charles H. Romine

Charles Romine is Director of the Information Technology Laboratory (ITL). ITL, one of seven research Laboratories within the National Institute of Standards and Technology (NIST), has an annual budget of $150 million, nearly 400 employees, and about 200 guest researchers from industry, universities, and foreign laboratories.

Dr. Romine oversees a research program cultivates trust in information technology and metrology by developing and disseminating standards, measurements, and testing for interoperability, security, usability, and reliability of information systems, including cybersecurity standards and guidelines for federal agencies and U.S. industry, supporting these and measurement science at NIST through fundamental and applied research in computer science, mathematics, and statistics. Through its efforts, ITL supports NIST's mission, to promote U.S. innovation and industrial competitiveness by advancing measurement science, standards, and technology in ways that enhance economic security and improve our quality of life.

Within NIST's traditional role as the overseer of the National Measurement System, ITL is conducting research addressing measurement challenges in information technology as well as issues of information and software quality, integrity, and usability. ITL is also charged with leading the Nation in using existing and emerging IT to help meet national priorities, including developing cybersecurity standards, guidelines, and associated methods and techniques, cloud computing, electronic voting, smart grid, homeland security applications, and health information technology.

Education:

Ph.D. in Applied Mathematics from the University of Virginia

B.A. in Mathematics from the University of Virginia.

Chairman LaHood. Thank you, Dr. Romine.

I now recognize Mr. Touhill for five minutes to present his testimony.

TESTIMONY OF MR. GREGORY J. TOUHILL, CISSP, CISM; BRIGADIER GENERAL, USAF (RET); ADJUNCT PROFESSOR, CYBERSECURITY & RISK MANAGEMENT, CARNEGIE MELLON UNIVERSITY, HEINZ COLLEGE

General Touhill. Thank you. Good morning, Chairman LaHood, Chairman Smith, Vice Chairman Abraham, Ranking Member Beyer, Ranking Member Lipinski, and members of the Committee. Thank you very much for the opportunity to appear today to discuss cyber risk management.

I'm retired Air Force Brigadier General Greg Touhill. I currently serve on the faculty of Carnegie Mellon University's Heinz College, where I instruct on cybersecurity and risk management. Prior to my current appointment, I served as the United States Chief Information Security Officer, and before that in the United States Department of Homeland Security, where I served as the Deputy Assistant Secretary for Cybersecurity and Communications. During that period, I also served as the Director of the National Cybersecurity and Communications Integration Center, which is commonly referred to by its acronym, NCCIC.

During my Air Force career, I served as one of the Air Force's first cyberspace operations officers, and I currently maintain both the Certified Information Systems Security Professional and Certified Information Security Manager professional certifications.

Cybersecurity is a risk management issue. However, many people mistakenly view it solely as a technology concern. Cybersecurity indeed is a multidisciplinary risk management issue and is an essential part of an enterprise risk management program.

I recognize we have a very full agenda of topics today, and I'm sensitive to your time. I have submitted for the record a written statement, and in that statement, I discuss the recent WannaCry attack and my assessment of how future attacks may impact the public and private sectors. In short, I view WannaCry as a slow-pitched softball whereas the next one may be a high-and-tight fastball coming in. We need to be ready.

I also discuss and share recommendations on topics the Committee has identified for today's agenda including the President's recent Cybersecurity Executive Order, public and private sector partnerships, the Cybersecurity Framework, and proposed legislation. In short, on that I urge the Congress to continue its great efforts to strengthen our enterprise risk posture. I urge you to authorize and empower the federal Chief Information Security Officer position, which currently is not an authorized or specified position. I also suggest that instead of calling it the NIST Cybersecurity Framework—and I'm a huge fan of this Framework—I suggest we start calling it the National Cybersecurity Framework to reinforce the fact that it applies to everyone, and further, NIST did a brilliant job in crowdsourcing the development of this framework but it was really people from around the country that brought to the table best practices. NIST was a great trail boss for this but it really is a national cybersecurity framework.

And then finally, in regards to the proposed H.R. 1224 legislation, I congratulate the Committee and the Members of the Congress for taking the initiative to really reinforce the need to implement the Framework across the federal government.

I do suggest, based upon my experience in both the military and the government sectors of the federal government, that we do two things with that Act. One is we amend that Act to make it apply to national security systems as well. Having served extensively in the military and in the federal government, I believe that the National Cybersecurity Framework applies equally to national security systems, and I recommend that you make that amendment. Further, I concur with my colleagues who suggest that let's leverage the Inspector General and auditing communities that are currently in the different departments and agencies and reinforce their need to conduct appropriate audits using that Cybersecurity Framework.

Again, I thank you for inviting me to discuss cyber risk management with you today, and I look forward to addressing any questions you may have.

[The prepared statement of General Touhill follows:]

Written Statement of Brigadier General (ret) Gregory J. Touhill
U.S. House of Representatives
Committee on Science, Space, & Technology
Hearing on "Ransomware and whether or to what extent the May 11th
Executive Order, NIST Framework, or Private Sector Could Assist in
Preventing Future Attacks."
Washington, DC
June 15, 2017

Good morning, Chairman Smith, Ranking Member Johnson, and Members of the committee. Thank you for the opportunity to appear here today to discuss cyber risk management.

I am retired Air Force Brigadier General Greg Touhill. I currently serve on the faculty of the Carnegie Mellon University's Heinz College, where I instruct on Cybersecurity and Risk Management. I appear today at the invitation of the committee and am testifying on my own behalf.

Prior to my current appointment, I served as the United States Chief Information Security Officer in the Executive Office of the President and, before that, in the U.S. Department of Homeland Security, where I served as the Deputy Assistant Secretary for Cybersecurity and Communications. During that period I also served as the Director of the National Cybersecurity and Communications Integration Center (NCCIC), commonly referred to by its acronym, "N-KICK".

During my Air Force career, I served as one of the Air Force's first cyberspace operations officers and was the 81st Training Wing commander where my team and I created the Air Force's cyberspace operations training programs for officers and enlisted personnel. I maintain both the Certified Information Systems Security Professional and Certified Information Security Manager professional certifications.

Cybersecurity is a risk management issue. Many people mistakenly view it solely as a technology problem. Cybersecurity is a multi-disciplinary risk management issue and is an essential part of an enterprise risk management program.

The recent Wannacry ransomware attack highlights the risk exposure many entities in both public and private sector accept when they do not implement best practices. Last month we saw many entities around the world fall victim to the consequences of Wannacry because they did not practice widely recognized best practices, such as keeping their hardware, software and network security procedures up-to-date in today's ever-evolving threat environment.

While Wannacry had severe impacts to many organizations around the world, it could have been much, much worse.

Wannacry did not incorporate what we call a classic "zero day" attack, where there is no advance warning. In fact, had the victim organizations updated their systems upon the initial warnings from entities like the US Cyber Emergency Readiness Team (USCERT), the FBI's Infragard program, Carnegie-Mellon's C-CERT, and private organizations such as the ISC2, ISACA, and the Center for Internet Security, I believe it is likely for the vast majority of victims that the attack could have been averted.

Systems using unpatched versions of the Windows 95 operating system have been highlighted as exemplar victims of the Wannacry attack. Microsoft who, after a long and very public notification process, discontinued support to the Windows 95 operating system in 2014, about 19 years after its initial release. However, in light of the warnings and their own research, in March of this year Microsoft issued a rare emergency patch to Windows 95, nearly three years after they had discontinued support of the software. Despite these extraordinary actions, many organizations still did not heed the warnings and properly patch and configure their systems. As a result, they fell victim to Wannacry.

The lesson here is that in today's highly-connected Internet-enabled world, our national prosperity and national security require us to ensure that we adhere to best practices to better manage our enterprise risk. One of those best practices is to keep our systems, both hardware and software, properly maintained and configured. In my view, this is a matter of due care and due diligence.

Regrettably, despite numerous warnings about aging hardware and software systems, both public and private sector organizations continue to accept significant risk by operating technically antique systems and unsupported software vulnerable to exploitation by hackers and other criminal groups.

The risk continues to grow as all aspects of our society, including our critical infrastructure, national economy, and even societal institutions, are reliant on a safe and secure Internet that is always on-line and available.

We got lucky with Wannacry. While warnings to update systems helped many harden their systems, many failed to do so and fell victim to the Wannacry ransomware. Fortunately, a cyber researcher discovered the Wannacry code contained an instruction that told the program to cease functioning if it made contact with a designated web site. Such sites are often used to provide command and control to the malicious software. The instruction found by the researcher is a rudimentary "kill switch" type of command that often is used by programmers to create a means of stopping a program or process.[i] The researcher found that the domain had not yet been registered and, for less than $11USD, created the domain. Once the domain was created, Wannacry-infected devices made contact with the domain, received a response that the domain was active, and the Wannacry program terminated on the infected devices per its instructions. Most programs are not written like Wannacry and aren't so easy to stop. We were lucky.

I believe Wannacry was a slow-pitch softball while the next attack is likely to be a blazing fastball. This time we anticipated an attack and issued warnings with valuable practical advice to mitigate it. The creators of Wannacry overtly placed a "kill switch" instruction set in the program's code. A researcher discovered and implemented that "kill switch" quickly to interrupt the attack. Next time I do not believe we will be so lucky.

We need to step up our game and take immediate actions across both the public and private sectors to better manage our cyber risk before the really fast pitches come flying into our networks.

I believe that stepping up our game includes building upon public-private sector partnerships and information sharing.

While I served as the Director of the National Cybersecurity and Communications Integration Center (NCCIC), I referred to our mission as being the lead for what I called the "National Cyber Neighborhood Watch". I believe that the "See Something, Say Something" concept applies to the cyber domain as it does to physical domains. Like our physical neighborhoods, when we see a problem, we need to point it out and share threat information and best practices to mitigate those threats with our neighbors. When we do so, we have a safer, more secure, and better Internet that promotes our national prosperity, our national security, and the values our society cherishes.

Sharing information about cyber threats, indicators of compromise, and best practices are essential parts of being responsible members of the "Cyber Neighborhood". I believe the US government is a leader in fostering public and private sector partnerships yet more work needs to be done to improve these partnerships so that all parties are satisfied with the relationships.

For example, I believe we need to relook at how we classify information. I found during my public sector career that well-intentioned government entities over-classify information. That stifles the timely sharing of information in an environment that already moves at light speed. Regrettably, some elements of the government hoard information that would be invaluable to America's critical infrastructure and other elements of the government. They do so under the guise of "protecting sources and methods." I found the bulk of classified indicators of compromise that came to my team in the NCCIC could be found on the Internet within days of our receiving it. I believe we ought to relook how we classify information and, instead of making the highest classification the default setting for data collection and dissemination, we ought to flip the default to a shareable setting. Classification at the highest level should not be the default setting; it should be the result of a deliberate determination by appropriate authorities that the information indeed is sensitive.

Sharing of information goes both ways. I thank the Congress for the creation of the Cybersecurity Information Sharing Act of 2015, which specified that private sector entities would not be penalized for sharing with the federal government and incorporated privacy provisions. This legislation was extremely helpful in providing "top cover" for programs such as the creation and fielding of the Automated Indicator Sharing (AIS) system developed by DHS. This system shares information about cyber threats between subscribers at machine speeds, reducing risk exposure to known threats. At the time of my departure from public service, over 3000 partners in the private sector had direct and indirect access to this capability. In essence, this technology took the time to share information from months to milliseconds.

While AIS is a welcome technology to improve public-private partnerships, it should not be viewed as the only means of sharing information. I view human relationships as critical. For example, while I was at DHS I engaged in monthly meetings with industry groups such as the Information Technology Sector Coordinating Council. I believe we need to encourage and remove impediments to direct engagement with industry leaders that will improve sharing of best practice information from experts in the private sector while providing those we serve with an open and transparent government. Teamwork is essential and the worst time to exchange business cards is during a crisis.

In all my many engagements as the US CISO, DHS Deputy Assistant Secretary, and NCCIC Director, I have been a huge proponent of incorporating the Framework for Improving Critical Infrastructure Cybersecurity into enterprise risk management programs in both the public and private sectors. I still am.

A framework is a basic structure underlying a system or methodology for solving a problem. For cyber risk management, our National Cybersecurity Risk Framework promotes a best practices-based methodology focused on:

1. **Identify**ing your assets and the threats against them
2. **Protect**ing against those threats based on your risk appetite
3. Being able to **Detect** when you are under attack or exceeding tolerable risk levels
4. Being able to **Respond** appropriately
5. Building in resiliency so that you can **Recover** when your bad day occurs

This core risk framework is not just a great one for Cybersecurity. I submit it is a great framework for risk management in general.

Most people refer to it as the NIST Cybersecurity Risk Framework. I prefer to refer to it as the National Cybersecurity Risk Framework because, while the NIST led the team that created it, it truly was a crowd-sourced document that incorporates best practices from numerous organizations and citizens, including me. It wasn't developed just by NIST. It was developed through the open call for best practices that NIST so brilliantly led.

As such, I suggest we formally name it the National Cybersecurity Risk Framework to reinforce that it is a best practice framework applicable to all of us, regardless of whether we are in the public sector, the private sector, in academia, or even at home. Our core National Cybersecurity Risk Framework is the best one I've seen and we ought to widely adopt it to better help manage our risk posture.

I am pleased to see the Presidential Executive Order on Strengthening the Cybersecurity of Federal Networks and Critical Infrastructure issued by the president on May 11th acknowledges that cybersecurity is a risk management issue. I further am pleased that it directs agency heads to use the framework to manage the agency's cybersecurity risk. Moreover, I am delighted that the order calls for a more modern, secure and resilient architecture. The companion OMB Memorandum 17-25, issued on May 19th, gives solid guidance for measuring progress toward meeting goals specified in Section One of the Executive Order. Both of these documents build upon the substantive work accomplished in both the Bush and Obama administrations to improve our cybersecurity risk posture and set the stage for even greater improvements.

While the executive order and the OMB memorandum are positive measures taken by the executive branch, there are opportunities the Congress can act upon to further enhance our cybersecurity posture. For example, despite the position being recognized as a best practice in the private sector for over 20 years, the Congress has yet to formally recognize the Federal Chief Information Security Officer position nor give it the specific authorities it needs. While I served in the position, I leveraged the experiences of my long career in public service, personal relationships and delegated authorities in order to perform my duties successfully, but it could have been a lot easier with help from the Congress. I recommend the Congress formally specify the Federal Chief Information Officer position in the next version of the Federal Information Security Management Act or comparable legislation and grant specified authorities to better manage our cybersecurity risk.

I am pleased this committee recognizes the importance of cyber risk management and implementation of the cybersecurity risk framework to better manage and reduce our cyber risk exposure. I have read the proposed HR 1224 bill and applaud your intent to improve the federal government's cybersecurity posture. I believe Section 20A to direct implementation of the framework and creation of the Federal Working Group to develop meaningful metrics and public reporting is hugely important and exercises the oversight appropriate in this risk environment.

I do not believe Section 20B, as currently written hits the right target. I am pleased that the committee wisely recognizes the importance of audits and what I call, "following through". However, I submit the following recommendations for your consideration and our potential discussion today:

1. National Security Systems should not be exempt. Based on my experience as a cyber operator in both the .mil and .gov domains, I believe the risk framework applies equally to all systems, especially to national security systems. I would not exempt them from the provisions of this act.

2. NIST should not lead cyber preparedness audits. Preparedness is a measure of operational readiness. The NIST mission and culture is deliberately not aligned with operations nor auditing. NIST cyber experts do not have the culture, expertise, manpower, or resources to conduct or orchestrate effective auditing. Moreover, NIST is widely viewed as "an honest broker" in developing standards and promoting new technologies. Assigning NIST duties to oversee audits or compliance activities changes their writ and perceptions about NIST's current and future roles. One of my senior colleagues in government service believes such action will have what he calls, "a chilling effect" on many of the relationships NIST has within government and industry. Additionally, many of my colleagues in the public, private, and academic communities have commented that their current relationships with NIST are "learning" relationships based on a common quest to identify and incorporate best practices. Assigning NIST duties to lead auditing or compliance activities changes those relationship and not in a good way. I have had numerous senior colleagues confess to me it likely will inhibit or stifle the free exchange of information from public and private entities to NIST. I recommend that the Congress not assign auditing and compliance activities to NIST and consider alternative actions.

3. I recommend the Congress direct the existing Inspectors Generals and Auditing functions, as choreographed through the Council of the Inspectors General on Integrity and Efficiency (CIGIE), to implement the actions of section 20B. This community has the culture, expertise, and organizational function to execute the tasks specified in Section 20B of the proposed legislation. The CIGIE and its members already have been incorporating the National Cybersecurity Risk Framework as part of their assessment criteria in many of their inspections and audits. In 2016 during my tenure as the U.S. Chief Information

Security Officer, I had discussions with the CIGIE and its cyber committee leadership to synchronize the efforts of OMB and the CIGIE to assess the cybersecurity risk of the executive branch departments and agencies. With the new executive order and companion OMB Memorandum 17-25, the stage is already set to follow-through on these efforts. I strongly urge the Congress to support these efforts by editing the proposed Section 20B to assign the proposed auditing and compliance actions from the NIST to the existing Inspectors Generals and auditing functions.

Again, I thank you for inviting me to discuss cyber risk management with you today. I look forward to addressing any questions you may have.

---

[i] Many researchers, academics, and practioners cite the 1988 Morris Worm incident as a reason why programmers should install a "kill switch" in the event that their program goes "out of control." See the following for more information on the Morris worm: https://www.washingtonpost.com/news/the-switch/wp/2013/11/01/how-a-grad-student-trying-to-build-the-first-botnet-brought-the-Internet-to-its-knees/?utm_term=.e38dbbf0a2c0

Brigadier General (ret) Greg Touhill

Greg Touhill is one of the nation's premier cybersecurity and information technology senior executives. A highly experienced leader of large, complex, diverse, and global operations, in 2016 Greg was selected by President Obama as the U.S. government's first Chief Information Security Officer. His other civilian government service includes duties as Deputy Assistant Secretary for Cybersecurity and Communications in the U.S. Department of Homeland Security and as Director of the National Cybersecurity and Communications Integration Center where he led national programs to protect the United States and its critical infrastructure. Greg is a retired Air Force general officer, a highly-decorated combat leader, an accomplished author and public speaker, a former American diplomat, and a senior executive with documented high levels of success on the battlefield and in the boardroom. He now serves as a faculty member at the Carnegie Mellon University's Heinz College, where he is the principal Cybersecurity and Risk Management instructor for the Chief Information Security Officer certification program.

Chairman LaHood. Thank you, Mr. Touhill.

I now recognize Dr. Thompson for five minutes to present his testimony.

TESTIMONY OF DR. HUGH THOMPSON, CHIEF TECHNOLOGY OFFICER, SYMANTEC

Mr. Thompson. Good morning. Thanks for having me, and Chairman LaHood, Vice Chairman Abraham, Chairman Smith, Ranking
Member Lipinski, and Ranking Member Beyer, I really appreciate
the opportunity to be here today to talk about what is a critical
subject.

Understanding the current threat environment is essential to
crafting good policy and effective defenses, and last month's
WannaCry ransomware attack is just one of the latest manifesta-
tions of the kinds of disruptive attacks that we are now facing.

The timeline of WannaCry I think has been well covered by the
other folks on this panel, but I did want to share with you a graph-
ical timeline that hopefully you can see in the monitor. Apologies
for the small print. What's interesting I think about that and
where I'd like to add some color is to give you Symantec's perspective on the events as they unfolded, and to give you some context,
Symantec is the world's largest cybersecurity company with technology protecting over 90 percent of the Fortune 500 and being
used extensively by government agencies around the world. In addition, we protect tens of millions of home users through our Norton and LifeLock branded products.

The threat telemetry we get from these deployments represents
the largest civilian threat intelligence network in the world.
WannaCry was unique and dangerous because of how quickly it
could spread. It was the first ransomware as a worm that had such
a rapid global impact. Once on a system, it propagated autonomously by exploiting a vulnerability in Microsoft Windows. After
gaining access to a computer, WannaCry installs the ransomware
package. This payload works in the same fashion as most crypto-
ransomware. It finds and encrypts a range of files and then displays essentially a ransom note to victims demanding payment,
this time in Bitcoin. Symantec worked closely with the U.S. Government from the first hours of the outbreak. We connected DHS
researchers with our experts, provided indicators of compromise
and analysis to DHS, and received the same back. During the outbreak, DHS had twice-daily calls with private sector to coordinate
operational activities. From our perspective, this was one of the
most successful public-private collaborations that we've been involved in.

Our analysis of WannaCry revealed that some of the tools and
infrastructure it used have strong links to a group referred to as
Lazarus by the security community, which the FBI has connected
with North Korea. Lazarus was linked to the destructive attacks
against Sony Pictures in 2014 and also the theft of approximately
$81 million from the Bangladesh Central Bank last year. The links
we saw between WannaCry and Lazarus included shared code, the
reuse of IP addresses, and similar code obfuscation techniques. As
a result, we believe it is highly likely that the Lazarus group was
behind the spread of WannaCry.

Beyond WannaCry, the threat landscape continues to evolve very quickly. We're seeing attacks become more sophisticated, not just in technology but in social engineering approaches that these attacks use. We're also seeing more attacks being leveraged against IOT devices such as the massive weaponization of IOT devices that we saw the Mirai botnet last fall. Mirai launched one of the largest distributed denial-of-service attacks on record and led to significant disruption of major cloud services. The explosive growth of attacks like WannaCry and Mirai I think underscores the need for preparation and deploying integrated and layered defenses.

These attacks also show the response and recovery planning and tools is an essential part of cyber risk management because when good defenses will stop many attacks, we have to be prepared that a determined adversary may get through those initial defenses and we must lay a foundation for recovery.

There's no question that WannaCry was an important event but unfortunately, it will not be the last of its kind. In fact, it's more likely an indicator of what's to come. Good fortune played a significant role in minimizing its impact, particularly in the United States, but we will not always have luck on our side, which is why we must learn the lessons of WannaCry and make the necessary improvements to our defenses and response capabilities.

This hearing is an important part of that effort, and we appreciate the opportunity to be here. I look forward to answering any questions that you may have. Thank you.

[The prepared statement of Mr. Thompson follows:]

Prepared Testimony and
Statement for the Record of

Hugh Thompson
Chief Technology Officer

Hearing on

"Bolstering the Government's Cybersecurity: Lessons Learned from WannaCry"

Before the

United States House of Representatives
Committee on Science, Space, and Technology
Subcommittee on Oversight
and
Subcommittee on Research and Technology

June 15, 2017

Chairman Comstock, Ranking Member Lipinski, Chairman LaHood, Ranking Member Beyer, my name is Dr. Hugh Thompson and I am the Chief Technology Officer (CTO) at Symantec. As CTO of the largest cybersecurity company in the world, I report directly to our CEO and am responsible for Symantec's long-term cybersecurity technology strategy. I have more than 15 years of experience in the security information space and have worked with many of the world's largest organizations and agencies on methodologies to make their systems more secure systems. In addition, I have authored three books and written more than 80 academic and industrial publications on security. For the last eight years I have served as the program committee chairman for the RSA Conference, which is the world's largest information security conference that brings together over 40,000 security professionals across the globe. I hold a Ph.D. in applied mathematics from the Florida Institute of Technology and for many years served as an adjunct professor at Columbia University in New York.

Symantec Corporation is the world's leading cybersecurity company, and has the largest civilian threat collection network in the world. Our Global Intelligence Network monitors over 175 million endpoints located in over 157 countries and territories. Additionally, we process more than 2 billion emails and billions of web requests each day. We maintain nine Security Response Centers and six Security Operations Centers around the globe, and all of these resources combined give our analysts a unique view of the entire cyber threat landscape.

Understanding the current threat environment is essential if we are going to craft good policy and effective defenses. And no recent threat has challenged our collective defenses or is more representative of today's evolving threat more than the WannaCry Ransomware outbreak last month. We are therefore pleased to see the Committee's continued interest in this subject, and appreciate the opportunity to provide our insights.

I.   **The Current and Emerging Cyber Threat Landscape**

Cyber attacks have reached new levels globally. Symantec recently released our 22nd Internet Security Threat Report,[1] which took an in-depth look at threats over the past year. In 2016 we saw explosive growth of ransomware, attempts to disrupt the US electoral process by state-sponsored groups, a record number of identities exposed in data breaches, and some of the biggest distributed denial of service (DDoS) attacks on record powered by a botnet of Internet of Things (IoT) devices. Yet while the attacks caused unprecedented levels of disruption and financial loss, perhaps the most striking feature of the current attack landscape is that in many cases attackers use very simple tools and tactics. During 2016, valuable Zero-day vulnerabilities and sophisticated malware was used more sparingly than in recent years. Instead, attackers increasingly attempted to hide in plain sight. They relied on straightforward approaches, such as spear-phishing emails and "living off the land" by using tools on hand, such as legitimate network administration software and operating system features. Yet despite this trend away from sophisticated attacks, the results were extraordinary, including:

- Over *1.1 billion* identities exposed;
- *Power outages* in the Ukraine;
- Over *$800 million* stolen through Business E-mail Compromise (BEC) scams over just a *six month period*;
- *$81 million* stolen in one bank heist alone;
- A *tripling* of the average ransomware demand;
- Average time-to-attack for a newly connected Internet of Thing device down to *two minutes*.

---

[1] See *Symantec Internet Security Threat Report*, XXII, April 2017

These shifting tactics demonstrate the resourcefulness of cyber criminals and attackers – but they also show that improved defenses and a concerted effort to address vulnerabilities can make a difference. Attackers are evolving and developing new attacks not because they want to, but because they have to do so. And that evolution comes with a financial cost to the attacker.

Ransomware continues to plague businesses and consumers, and due to its destructiveness is one of the most dangerous cybercrime threats we currently face. During 2016, criminal gangs engaged in indiscriminate campaigns involving massive volumes of malicious emails that in some cases overwhelmed organizations by the sheer volume of ransomware-laden emails alone. Attackers are demanding more and more from victims, and the average ransom demand *more than tripled* in 2016, from $294 to $1,077. The number of new ransomware families also more than tripled to 101, from 30 in both 2014 and 2015. The volume of attacks increased as well. Detections were up 36% percent from 2015, and by December we were seeing almost twice the daily volume that we observed in January.

We are also seeing the emergence of Ransomware-as-a-Service (RaaS). This involves malware developers creating ransomware kits, which can be used easily to create and customize new variants. Typically the developers provide the kits to attackers for a percentage of the proceeds. One example of RaaS is Shark (Ransom.SharkRaaS), which is distributed through its own website and allows users to customize the ransom amount and which files it encrypts. Payment is automated and sent directly to Shark's creators, who retain 20 percent and send the remainder on to the attackers. Our statistics show that, for the most part, attackers are concentrating their attacks on countries with developed, stable economies – 34% of the detections were in the US, and another 39% spread among the United Kingdom, Australia, Germany, Russia, the Netherlands, Canada, India, and Italy.

The world of cyber espionage experienced a notable shift towards more overt activity in 2016, much of which was designed to destabilize and disrupt targeted organizations and countries. We saw:

- a January 2016 attack against the Ukrainian power grid;
- an attack on the World Anti-Doping Agency and subsequent release of test results;
- a widespread, destructive attack on computers in Saudi Arabia; and
- a second attack against the Ukrainian power grid in December of 2016.

In years past, any one of these events would have been the biggest story of the year. But in 2016, we also saw an attack on the US Presidential election, an operation that the Intelligence Community (IC) attributed to Russia. Cyber attacks involving sabotage have traditionally been rare, but 2016 saw two separate waves of attacks involving destructive malware. Disk-wiping malware was used against targets in the attacks on the Ukraine in January and again in December, resulting in power outages. Additionally, a disk-wiping trojan known as Shamoon reappeared after a four-year absence and was used against multiple organizations in Saudi Arabia. Previously, Shamoon was used in highly destructive attacks against Saudi and other Middle Eastern energy companies, and press reports linked it to Iran.

In 2016, cyber criminals expanded their focus from individual bank customers to the banks themselves, sometimes attempting to steal tens of millions of dollars in a single attack. Two groups targeted the Society for Worldwide Interbank Financial Telecommunication (SWIFT) network and stole SWIFT credentials. They used those credentials to initiate fraudulent transactions and covered their tracks by doctoring the banks' printed confirmation messages to delay discovery of the transfers. One group began its attack at the start of a long weekend to reduce the likelihood of a quick discovery.

And while ransomware and financial fraud groups continue to pose the biggest threat to end users, other threats are beginning to emerge. It was only a matter of time before attacks on IoT devices began to gain momentum, and during 2016 Symantec witnessed a twofold increase in attempted attacks against IoT devices. 2016 also saw the first major incident originating from IoT devices, the Mirai botnet, which was composed of routers, digital video cameras, and security cameras. Weak security – in the form of default and hard-coded passwords – made these devices easy pickings for attackers. After compromising millions of devices, the attackers controlled a botnet big enough to carry out the largest DDoS attacks ever seen. In October, the combined power of these compromised devices led to brief outages at some of the most popular websites and online services in the world. Mirai's impact was further magnified when the developer released the source code for the malware, which led to copycat efforts by other groups.

II.   WannaCry Outbreak

The WannaCry ransomware outbreak began on Friday, May 12, 2017, and within hours it disrupted Britain's National Health Service (NHS) and Spanish telecom provider Telefonica. After a day, it had infected more than 230,000 computers in over 150 countries. At that point the infection rate plummeted, largely through good luck – a security researcher in the United Kingdom had unknowingly triggered a kill switch when he registered a domain name he found within the code of the ransomware. This prevented the worm from moving laterally, greatly slowing the spread of the infection and effectively halting the initial outbreak over the weekend. Still, over the course of three days (May 12-15), Symantec blocked WannaCry more than 22 million times on more than 300,000 devices. We were able to prevent WannaCry infections because we implemented protections for the underlying vulnerability in April (*See* Attachment for a complete timeline of WannaCry).

WannaCry was unique and dangerous because of how quickly it could spread. It is the first ransomware-as-a-worm that has had scaled global impact; once on a system it propagated autonomously using the Eternal Blue vulnerability in the Windows Server Messaging Block (SMB) protocol. After gaining access to a computer, WannaCry installs a backdoor implant tool called DoublePulsar which transfers and runs the WannaCry ransomware package. The payload works in the same fashion as most modern crypto-ransomware: it finds and encrypts a range of files, then displays a "ransom note" demanding a payment in bitcoin ($300 first week; $600 second week).

WannaCry spread to unpatched computers. Microsoft released a patch for the SMB vulnerability for Windows 7 and newer operating systems in March, but unpatched systems and systems running XP or older operating systems were unprotected. After the WannaCry outbreak began, Microsoft released a patch for XP and earlier platforms. Four days after the initial outbreak these patches were widely applied and new infections slowed to a trickle.

The US government reacted quickly to the outbreak. DHS's National Cybersecurity and Communications Integration Center (NCCIC) held twice daily calls with the private sector to coordinate operational activities. We participated, as did more than a dozen security and IT companies. During these calls, DHS representatives and the private sector shared Indicators of Compromise (IoCs), mitigation techniques, and information on threat vectors. In addition, the NCCIC distributed written analysis on the attack.

Symantec worked closely with the US government from the first hours of the outbreak. We connected DHS researchers with our experts, provided IoCs and analysis to DHS, and received the same from DHS. After the infection waned, we continued our partnership, sharing details about the Lazarus connections (detailed below) that that we were finding. From our perspective, this was one of the most successful public/private incident response efforts in which we have participated.

III.   Origins of WannaCry

Tools and infrastructure used in the WannaCry ransomware attacks have strong links to Lazarus, the group that was linked to the destructive attacks on Sony Pictures and the theft of $81 million from the

Bangladesh Central Bank. Our researchers discovered that prior to the global outbreak on May 12, an earlier version of WannaCry was used in a small number of targeted attacks in February, March, and April. These earlier versions of WannaCry used stolen credentials to spread across infected networks, rather than leveraging the Eternal Blue/SMB exploit that caused WannaCry to spread quickly across the globe starting on May 12. Our analysis of these early WannaCry attacks revealed substantial commonalities in the tools, techniques, and infrastructure used by the attackers and those seen in previous Lazarus attacks. This included shared code, reuse of IP addresses, and similar code obfuscation. Thus we believe it is highly likely that the Lazarus group was behind the spread of WannaCry. We do note, however, that the WannaCry attacks are in many ways more typical of a cyber crime campaign than they are of nation-state activity.

IV.   Public Private Partnerships

We partner with the US government, and governments around the world, in the fight against cybercrime and cyber attacks. The US Department of Homeland Security works with the private sector through a variety of programs, and has made considerable progress in recent years engaging with industry, especially in the area of information sharing. As noted above, the coordination between government and the private sector was on display during the response to WannaCry.

Some partnership programs are formal, such as the Cyber Information Sharing and Collaboration Program (CISCP). This is DHS's primary structure for private companies to share information about incidents, cyber threats and known vulnerabilities. For example, last October, we used the CISCP program to share a report we published that exposed one of the groups that was trying to steal money from banks by exploiting the SWIFT messaging system. Through CISCP, we passed along our in-depth, technical research to CISCP managers along with a list of indicators including hashes, command and control nodes, and domains. The CISCP team then used our indicators to create an Indicator Bulletin (IB) and pushed it out to all CISCP participants for their use.

In addition to the Department's formal programs, we work with DHS informally. For instance, earlier this year we hosted a group of ten cyber threat analysts at our Herndon Security Operations Center to discuss specific threats and to explore potential areas to coordinate in the future. Among other topics, we discussed Shamoon, a family of destructive malware that we have tracked for years. Shamoon was used in attacks against the Saudi energy sector in 2012 and last year we tracked a fresh wave of attacks hitting the Middle East. The opportunity to sit face-to-face and discuss threats often alleviates a chief concern among many private sector security companies, that too often the information flows just one way – from industry to the government. In-person exchanges often lead to a more complete and bilateral interchange of ideas.

Partnerships can lead to concrete results. One recent example came in December 2016, when Symantec concluded a decade-long research campaign that helped unearth an international cybercriminal gang dubbed "Bayrob." The group is responsible for stealing up to $35 million from victims through auto auction scams, credit card fraud and computer intrusions. Through our research, we discovered multiple versions of Bayrob malware, collected voluminous intelligence data, and tracked Bayrob as it morphed from online fraud to a botnet consisting of over 300,000 computers used primarily for cryptocurrency mining. Over time, Symantec's research team gained deep technical insight into Bayrob's operations and its malicious activities, including its recruitment of money mules. These investigations and countermeasures were crucial in assisting the Federal Bureau of Investigation (FBI) and authorities in Romania in building their case to arrest three of Bayrob's key actors and extradite them to the U.S. They are currently in federal custody awaiting trial.

The private sector is also working together to counter cybercrime and industry partnerships have proven highly effective in fighting cybercrime. The Cyber Threat Alliance (CTA) is an excellent example of the private sector banding together to improve the overall safety and security of the Internet. In 2014, Symantec, Fortinet, Intel Security, and Palo Alto Networks formed the CTA to work together to share threat information. Since that time, Cisco and Checkpoint have joined the CTA as founding members. The goal of the CTA is to better distribute detailed information about advanced attacks and thereby raise the situational awareness of CTA members and improve overall protection for our customers.

Prior industry sharing efforts were often limited to the exchange of malware samples, and the CTA sought to change that. Over the past three years the CTA has consistently shared more actionable threat intelligence such as information on "zero day" vulnerabilities, command and control server information, mobile threats, and indicators of compromise related to advanced threats. By raising the industry's collective intelligence through these new data exchanges, CTA members have delivered greater security for individual customers and organizations.

Conclusion

WannaCry was an important event – but it will not be the last of its kind. Thankfully, the outbreak was stopped before it caused major global damage, but this was as much through good fortune as it was through what was a largely effective response. Learning the lessons of WannaCry and improving our ability to respond is essential, because the next attack is coming. We are pleased to help the Committee in doing so, and this hearing is an important part of that effort.

Attachment:

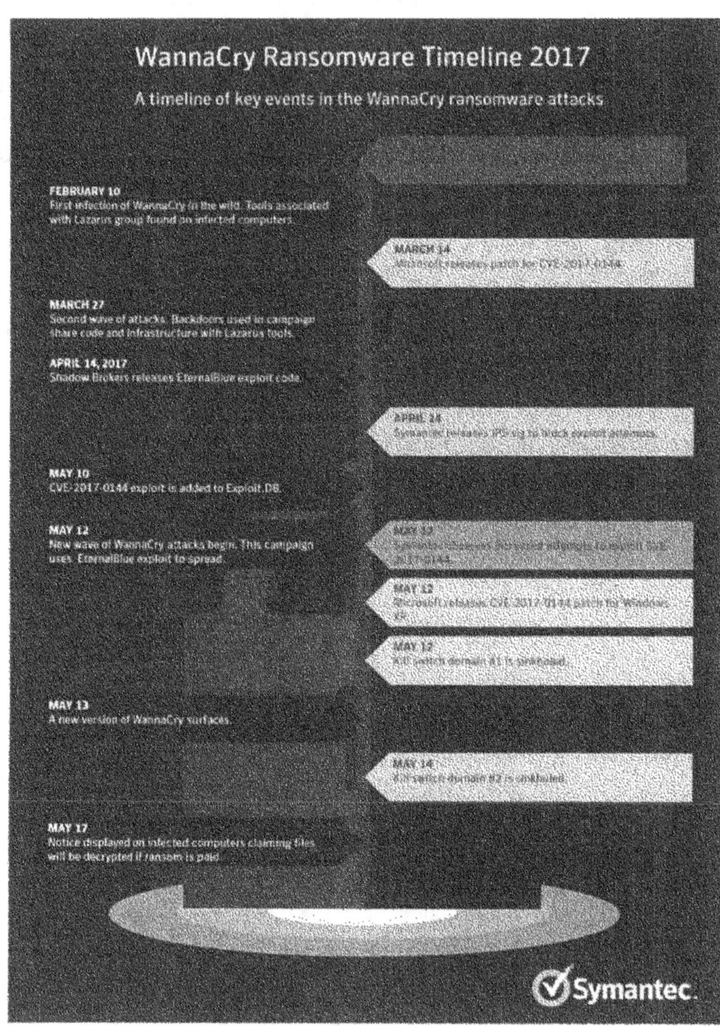

WannaCry Ransomware Timeline 2017
A timeline of key events in the WannaCry ransomware attacks
FEBRUARY 10
First infection of WannaCry in the wild. Tools associated with Lazarus group found on infected computers.
MARCH 14
Microsoft releases patch for CVE-2017-0144.
MARCH 27
Second wave of attacks. Backdoors used in campaign share code and infrastructure with Lazarus tools.
APRIL 14, 2017
Shadow Brokers releases EternalBlue exploit code.
APRIL 24
Symantec releases IPS sig to block exploit attempts.
MAY 10
CVE-2017-0144 exploit is added to Exploit.DB.
MAY 12
New wave of WannaCry attacks begin. This campaign uses EternalBlue exploit to spread.
MAY 12
Symantec observes increased attempts to exploit CVE-2017-0144.
MAY 12
Microsoft releases CVE-2017-0144 patch for Windows XP.
MAY 12
Kill switch domain #1 is sinkholed.
MAY 13
A new version of WannaCry surfaces.
MAY 14
Kill switch domain #2 is sinkholed.
MAY 17
Notice displayed on infected computers claiming files will be decrypted if ransom is paid.
Symantec.

Hugh Thompson
Senior Vice President, Chief Technology Officer
Symantec Corporation

Dr. Hugh Thompson is a leading force in the information security industry. He has co-authored four books, written more than 80 academic and industrial publications on security, has been a contributor to The New York Times, and has been interviewed by top news organizations including the BBC, CNN, NPR, Financial Times, Washington Post, Forbes, The Wall Street Journal, and others. He has more than a decade of experience creating methodologies that help organizations build demonstrably more secure systems. He joined Blue Coat in 2012 and served as CTO & CMO until the acquisition of Blue Coat by Symantec in August 2016. Dr. Thompson is now CTO of Symantec and leads the researchers and architects in the Office of the CTO and is also responsible for additional areas such as analyst relations.

In 2006, Dr. Thompson was named one of the "Top 5 Most Influential Thinkers in IT Security" by SC Magazine and has, for the past several years, served as the program committee chairman for RSA Conference, guiding the technical content for the world's largest information security gathering. He previously sat on the Editorial Board of IEEE Security and Privacy Magazine, and served as an adjunct professor at Columbia University in New York for many years. Dr. Thompson holds a B.S., M.S. and Ph.D. in applied mathematics from the Florida Institute of Technology.

v. 4-17

Chairman LaHood. Thank you, Dr. Thompson, and thank all the witnesses for your testimony. The Chair recognizes himself for five minutes, and we'll begin questioning.

As I talked about in the beginning, the title of this hearing today is "Lessons Learned from WannaCry," and we've talked a lot this morning about WannaCry and how that played out across the world, but in terms of what we've learned about the genesis and origin of where this came from, I know the Washington Post came out with an article yesterday that the NSA has linked the WannaCry computer worm to North Korea. I'm wondering if, Dr. Neino, you can talk a little bit about the genesis and origin of where this came from, particularly because it appears it's from a nation-state, and I know there's references to what occurred with Sony Pictures and also with the Bangladesh Bank, and what we know about it and what's being implemented I guess on the government side to prevent this or hold an entity or the government accountable.

Mr. Neino. Thank you, Chairman. I think if I understand your question, you're asking about, one, the origin, and our conjecture to that, and number two, perhaps, if I understood also correctly, what would be the rules of engagement for something like that if it was another nation-state. While I may not be—while we think it's ambiguous to conjecture over the origins of WannaCry, there are tails of code in there that suggest one way or another that some nation-state could have been responsible. Unfortunately, and as I said in my written testimony, anyone could have created this level of attack, and often misdirection is found typically in binaries like these attacks we see. I would compare it perhaps an analogy to photoshopping a program to look a certain way or it could have simply just been what it is, which is exactly what we see. It's hard to tell so we won't—I won't say that I know the origin of the attack nor should I conjecture on it but what I can say is that these attacks are very difficult to attribute, and Kryptos Logic is a cybersecurity company, not an intelligence agency, so it would be very difficult for us to pursue an answer to that.

As far as rules of engagement, I also think that the question segues the same way. It would be difficult to create attribution or origin to any attack and therefore rules of engagement would be very difficult for us to give any kind of assessment on.

Chairman LaHood. Dr. Thompson?

Mr. Thompson. This was truly an interesting attack. We spend a lot of time in our research labs looking at both the code that was used in WannaCry but also where WannaCry communicated out to, and there were very, very close similarities to other kinds of attacks that we've seen, specifically attacks that we attribute to a group called Lazarus, and these attacks, this malware, the reuse of strings in that malware, the reuse of command-and-control infrastructure out on the internet by that malware led our researchers to believe that this is strongly linked to the Lazarus group.

Now, similar to my colleague on the end, we're not the intelligence community either, and I agree with those comments that attribution is often difficult, but what we've seen leads us to believe that it was a part of this Lazarus Group and separately the FBI has linked the Lazarus group with North Korea, and I think,

Chairman LaHood, the article that you're referring to from yesterday is another potential evidence point on that as well from the NSA.

Chairman LaHood. Thank you.

Dr. Neino, we talked about the kill switch and how that stopped the attack, but we also reference the fact that last week a hospital on the East Coast and a high school were subject to attack. Can you explain how if the kill switch was implemented correctly, how the hackers responsible for WannaCry were able to continue to perpetuate the attack despite the registration of the kill switch.

Mr. Neino. Absolutely. Although I'd like to be a doctor, it's Mr. Neino.

So you have to understand the material makeup of the actual malware and how it works. Why WannaCry was so significant is that it's self-propagating. That's what gives it the title a worm, if you will, meaning the actors don't need to even be in existence, and sometimes we refer to these things as zombies, zombie botnets, because they continue to proliferate regardless of the actors or parents or creators of the particular attack. In the case of the examples I gave in the testimony regarding the health system, of which there are many, that was just, let's say, a corner case that was very significant. The worm continues to propagate because it is scanning and seeking to expand itself, and that portion of the worm is not subject to the kill switch so its expansion and spreading which in effect is still exploiting systems worldwide. What it's not triggering is the payload, if you will, the ransom component, and that component therefore doesn't trigger. Most of these organizations worldwide right don't know they're getting actively exploited still because it's because they don't see the ransom portion of it, so that's why we have 60 million attacks thwarted to date, if not more, and just nobody knows it's still happening, and that's why I said it was—I don't think the message has resonated given those figures that this still needs to be patched and this again points to the point of resources.

Chairman LaHood. Thank you, Mr. Neino.

I'm out of time. I will yield to the Ranking Member, Mr. Beyer.

Mr. Beyer. Thank you, Chairman LaHood, very much, and I'm so impressed by our panel today. There's so much information here, and I congratulate Dr. Romine and Dr. Thompson for being Ph.D. mathematicians. That's wonderful. Jerry McNerney was here just a little while ago, a Member of Congress, who's I believe our only mathematician in Congress. And Mr. Neino, congratulations on winning the hacking tournament. I never had a chance to say that before, but that's very cool. And General Touhill, it's very cool that you're now after all the things you've done in your life, combat and diplomacy and first CISO to be up there at Carnegie Mellon with their buggy races around Chandlee Park. Every university has something that makes them cooler than everyplace else.

And General, I want to start with you. You talked in your long written testimony about H.R. 1224 cosponsored by—a bipartisan bill here, but we have expressed a lot of concern about the audit function that NIST would be asked to take on, and I was particularly fascinated by your points which we didn't raise when we had the hearing here that it would make it much more difficult for

NIST to be viewed as an honest broker that this would change their perceptions about the current and future roles and have a chilling effect on many of the relationships that NIST has within government and industry that a lot of these relationships are, quote, unquote, learning relationships based on a common quest to identify and incorporate best practices, and NIST would change those relationships and not in a good way. It might inhibit or stifle the free exchange of information from public and private entities to NIST. Can you expand on that at all? This seems to be a pretty powerful argument against that audit function.

General TOUHILL. Yes, sir. You know, frankly, I'm a fan of the intent of the legislation. Section 20(a) in making sure that folks are in fact using the Cybersecurity Framework across federal government I think is brilliant. We need to follow through on that big time, and frankly, it was something I was promoting while I was the United States Chief Information Security Officer. As a matter of fact, in my last federal Chief Information Security Officer Council meeting in January of this year, I proposed and we had a unanimous vote amongst the council to do a risk assessment for the federal government based on the Framework. That portion of the legislation I'm wholly supportive of.

Section 20(b), the proposal to do the auditing and compliance activities, I'm also a fan of. I think it's important that we do auditing and compliance. However, I do stand by what I wrote in the written testimony that I think that NIST is not the best place to put that. It doesn't have the culture, it doesn't have the mission, it doesn't have the personnel to do it as effectively as the existing Inspector General and auditing functions. And from a practical standpoint, NIST is a great organization that I've been working with for the last 35-plus years, and the relationships that NIST has is in fact as a neutral party that is on the quest to choreograph efforts to find the best ways of doing things. An auditing function or a compliance function on the other hand is looking to see if you are in fact following the checklist. I think that if we want to have an auditing and compliance function, which I definitely think that we should be doing, we should be giving direction to those folks whose job it is to do that auditing and compliance function. Frankly, this is an operational issue, and Inspector Generals have always been in my book the folks that do performance inspections, that are the ones that are going to help those commanders in the field in the military as well as the executives in the federal government do their job better and have better visibility into their risk posture. I believe we need to have the Inspector Generals and auditing functions that are currently in place be the ones who execute the intent of the Committee and the Congress.

Mr. BEYER. Thank you, General, very much.

Mr. Neino, based on your testimony, you should be a doctor. It's filled with really interesting things, and your three-part conclusion that the largest issues were A, that organizations are too slow to adapt; B, that we have a vast human resource shortage; and C, there are little by way of metrics to demonstrate return on investment, and you talk about creating a method to prioritize threats, something like the Richter Scale, magnitude and a clear and repeatable scale. Who should put this together? Who should manage it? Who should maintain it? How do we make this happen?

Mr. NEINO. I think it would be interesting to see NIST participation in something of this where it's basically crowdsourced through various academics and commercial and private entities that could look together and see how they're prioritizing risks and threats, and then see if that could be in some way put into some sort of simulation system that allows to be scalable where people as a resource is not scalable, technology can be, and that would be an effective area.

I also see that the commercial sector alone can produce that as well and that could be adopted, but I think that any time you have some sort of regulatory mandate, it's taken much more seriously, and what I mean by that is, for instance, if we had an event of magnitude that was measured and if we put an arbitrary number on WannaCry, let's say it was a 7.5 magnitude by some arbitrary figure, shouldn't that particular event be required to be fixed by organizations whereas right now it's mostly voluntarily. So if a water system or a power grid doesn't fix it even after WannaCry, shouldn't we see that sort of mandate where we can know that that is regulated because that event of magnitude has context versus you can't boil the ocean when it comes to patching vulnerabilities. We're not going to win that war; it's infinite. But we should be able to win the war of at least the attacks we know about.

Mr. BEYER. Thank you very much.

Mr. Chair, I yield back.

Chairman LaHOOD. Thank you, Mr. Beyer.

I now recognize Vice Chairman Abraham.

Mr. ABRAHAM. Thank you, Mr. Chairman. I also stand in awe of the brain cell power on our panel. We could probably use a couple of guys as mathematicians when we work through our budget process.

And Dr. Thompson, if indeed North Korea has a role in this virus exploitation, I find it ironic that a country as North Korea that not only suppresses but quashes religious freedom would use a biblical name, Lazarus, as its codename, so just an aside.

Dr. Romine, my question is to you. When news of WannaCry started spreading, what, if any, steps did NIST take to ensure federal agencies information systems were protected and was NIST involved in any government meeting that took place around that time?

Dr. ROMINE. Thank you very much for the question. The response for an event like WannaCry from the NIST perspective, the primary goal as a scientific institution and as an institution that provides guidance is to learn as much as we can about the incident and about the origin—not the origin from a country point of view but the technical origins, and to determine whether the guidance that we issue is sufficiently robust to help organizations prevent this kind of attack.

I'm not aware of specific meetings that we were involved in that were discussing the operational side of WannaCry. I think the law enforcement and intelligence communities were certainly meeting. You heard reference to DHS being quite active in helping the private sector to deal with this issue. From our perspective, it's more learning whether we can improve the guidance that we make available to entities to try to not only prevent these attacks but also recover from them and to be prepared for them in the future.

Mr. ABRAHAM. Okay. And I'll stay with you for my second question. In your testimony, which I did read, you said that NIST recommendations in the NIST guide for the cybersecurity event recovery and Cybersecurity Framework would sufficiently address the WannaCry incidents. Will the requirement in the cyber Executive Order to agencies to implement the Framework help them be better prepared in the future to defend against these types of incidences and will this be enough or should more be done?

Dr. ROMINE. Thanks for the question. It's difficult to know whether it will be enough for the next event, but I can say this. One of the important things that emerged in our discussions with the private sector during the development of the Framework was that we are often thinking about detection and prevention of attacks. Sometimes, we don't pay enough attention to response and recovery, and so one of the things that the Framework does is to spell out the five functions—identify, protect, detect, respond and recover—and we're providing a lot of guidance now with the incident response guidance, for example, to help different organizations be better prepared to respond and recover. One of the analogies that I've drawn recently is the Boy and Girl Scouts are right: their motto is "be prepared." And the fact is, the better prepared an organization is through its risk management activities, which we think the risk management framework from FISMA coupled with for federal agencies and under the umbrella of the Cybersecurity Framework now, we think those are the tools that are necessary to implement the kind of preparedness that organizations should have.

Mr. ABRAHAM. One quick follow-up. What specific steps in lieu of this WannaCry should NIST take to help federal and state agencies be better prepared as well as the private sector?

Dr. ROMINE. So we're already looking at some of the consequences associated with it, some of the incident response work that we have, some of the data integrity work that I talked about earlier. We launched the Data Integrity Project at the National Cybersecurity Center of Excellence, which has a very strong tie-in with ransomware-type attacks. We launched that actually before the WannaCry came out but in light of this new event, we're accelerating the work that's going on in the NCCOE so we hope to be able to provide very practical guidance or practical examples of how to be prepared so that organizations can see how it's done.

Mr. ABRAHAM. Thank you.

And General, thank you for your service to the country.

Mr. Chairman, I yield back.

Chairman LAHOOD. Thank you, Vice Chairman Abraham.

I now recognize Ranking Member Lipinski for his questioning.

Mr. LIPINSKI. Thank you, Mr. Chairman. I want to thank the witnesses for their testimony and for all the work that you do.

We are I think finally beginning to take cybersecurity more seriously here in Washington although there's much more that I think we need to do. Part of the problem is understanding what this really means and the impact that it can have. We also need to make sure that the American public knows the significance of cybersecurity and what could happen.

We know when we're dealing with cybersecurity that technology is just part of the solution. What often matters more is we saw with WannaCry is personal behavior and organizational behavior. Individuals and information systems managers must regularly install security patches and phase out outdated software. Organizations must prioritize cybersecurity and have plans in place for quick response when there are attacks. These are social-science issues.

Another social-science angle is understanding criminal and terror networks as well as foreign state actors, and using that understanding to help inform our intelligence gathering and our cyber defenses.

So I'd like to hear from each of our witnesses your thoughts on whether we're investing enough in the human factors of cybersecurity and what more can be done, what more would you like to see us do to—so that we are taking care of these issues? We'll start with Mr. Neino.

Mr. NEINO. Thank you, Mr. Lipinski. I think it's a great point that you bring up. There are other issues other than technology at play. Cybersecurity is hard. It really is. Software is hard; security is hard. When you put them together, it's very hard. One thing that we know will be quite difficult is resources. Resources will maintain their need for quite some time, and technology is rapidly evolving. We have eroding boundaries. Systems are changing. We have digital transformation that continuously happens so we have to relearn our resources and people. This makes it very difficult for those responsible in those areas to manage risk to actually keep up with the actual threat, the pragmatic threat, not just the way we measure our own threats but in reality like WannaCry. In that case, I think that we could see a huge value if we were to see investments in things that allow for threat prioritization, again going back to the events of magnitude example. You can't boil the ocean but you can look at the areas that can hurt you the most and the people that will hurt you the most, and investigating those things and putting them together allows you to start to formulate a picture that allows you to prioritize threats. Once you prioritize threats, the investments you make in those people and those resources will be maximized and we'll have a better chance of being more resilient.

Mr. LIPINSKI. Thank you.

Dr. Romine?

Dr. ROMINE. I'd like to describe two important NIST programs that directly address the human part of this problem. One is that NIST is privileged to home the program office for the National Initiative for Cybersecurity Education, or NICE, which is an interagency program that's dedicated to building a larger cybersecurity workforce, and we've made great strides in that area. I'm very proud of the work that we've done there.

The second part of the program is, and you're absolutely right, that one of the key components in achieving true security is understanding how humans interact with technology. You can be theoretically secure through technology but if the people that are trying to get their jobs done are focused on that and not taking advantage of, or in some cases, even circumventing security that's in place in order to get their jobs done, you have to know about that and you have to understand how to build systems that have the human in the loop. NIST views a systems-level approach for cybersecurity but we think people, the users, are part of the system and so we have an active research program in understanding. We have psychologists, sociologists, human factors engineers on our staff whose entire mission is to understand how people interact with technology so that we can do better in areas like security and usability.

Mr. LIPINSKI. General Touhill?

General TOUHILL. Thank you very much. When I was at—still in public service as the U.S. Chief Information Security Officer, I applied about five strategic lines of effort. One was harden the workforce; two, treat information as an asset; three, do the right things the right way and at the right time; four, make sure that you're continuously innovating and investing wisely; and then five; make sure that you're making risk management decisions at the right level.

The first one was harden the workforce. If you gave me an extra dollar in cybersecurity, I'm always going to spend it on people, and frankly, your people are your greatest resource but they're also your weakest link. We see it time and time again, and 95 percent of the incidents my U.S. ICS, Industry Control System CERTs responded to you could track back to a human failure—failure to patch, failure to configure correctly, failure to read the instruction book. So I think hardening the workforce should be a strategic priority, and it was one of my top ones and actually was the top one.

Further, you know, if you ask for where else could we invest well: exercises. People should not necessarily be confronting crises without having practiced ahead of time, and my friend, Admiral Thad Allen, likes to say the time to exchange business cards is not a time of crisis. We should be doing exercises more often than we are, and we should be investing more into them.

And then further, everybody needs to play. Too often we see senior executives who go dismiss that off to the younger folks and the kids in the server room to play. It's a risk issue, and risk decisions are made at the board level.

So I think we need to invest in exercises. We already are doing a lot. During the time I was at DHS when I first got there, the year before we had done 44. By the time I left two years later, we were up to 270 exercises. But I think more needs to be done, and I encourage the Committee and the Congress to help reward these type of practices because I think it'll buy down our risk.

Mr. LIPINSKI. And if the Chairman will indulge me, Dr. Thompson?

Mr. THOMPSON. Thank you. Thanks for that question because I think what you're hitting on is probably one of the most important and underinvested areas in cybersecurity in general. This human element cannot be separated from the technology. Often in the security community we talk about advanced persistent threats, and most people when they think about that think about very sophisticated code, malware, but in fact, what we're seeing is the root of many of these advanced persistent threats is the initial way a company got infected or a person got infected was that an individual made in retrospect a bad choice—they clicked on a link, they downloaded a file—and we're seeing attackers becoming more socially sophisticated in the way they attack. We're seeing them personalize attacks looking for information on social networking sites, for example, so that they can create credibility in an email or a text message that they may send you so that you're convinced that this is a reasonable thing to go and do. And I think from an industry perspective, it is a place that we desperately need focus.

I want to give you one data point that I think may be useful. So I've had the pleasure to serve as the program committee chairman for RSA Conference for the past ten years. That conference had 40,000 people, security professionals that showed up last year, which is a sign of how important I think this industry's become, and three years ago we started a track called the Human Element, and it has become one of the most popular tracks for cybersecurity professionals because I think we all realize—and I love the comments that the general made about this topic. I think we all realize that is one of the most critical areas that we need to focus on going forward, human element of the people that are responsible for cybersecurity but also the human element of users.

And I'll make a final comment here. It is very easy for a user to understand that there's an increase in utility. I know it's easier to get in my house if I leave the door unlocked, very easy. You don't have to carry any keys around. If I make it more secure, generally people's viewpoint is you make it more secure, you make it more painful. There are more things that you have to do. So they can easily measure utility but they can't easily measure risk, and we need to do a better job at helping the individual, the citizen recognize risk.

Mr. LIPINSKI. Thank you very much.

Chairman LaHOOD. Thank you, Mr. Lipinski.

I now recognize Congressman Higgins for his questions.

Mr. HIGGINS. Thank you, Mr. Chairman.

Mr. Neino, congratulations on shutting down WannaCry. That was a big mistake by whoever designed that worm, was it not, to leave the domain unregistered?

Mr. NEINO. It's hard to say what it is. It could have been intentional, it could have been non-intentional. We think it was non-intentional but it's hard to say. But it definitely was a mistake in any regard.

Mr. HIGGINS. Well, congratulations on discovering it. What would WannaCry had done to the world had that kill switch not been——

Mr. NEINO. I can only give a thumbnail of what that might look like but given today, you know, we're seeing millions of thwarted attacks per day, you also have to realize that the velocity of the attack of WannaCry had slowed significantly as a result of the kill switch. So generally mathematicians will say these are exponential attacks, things like that. This could have been a very, very massive attack. Most systems were affected.

Mr. HIGGINS. I concur. Most cyber experts agree that it appears that North Korea was behind WannaCry. Do you agree?

Mr. NEINO. I think that there are tails in the software program that you could use to associate it but I do believe that intelligence is cumulative behind cyber. Cyber is very difficult to attribute. You need other areas to attribute a——

Mr. HIGGINS. What's your opinion? Was North Korea behind WannaCry?

Mr. NEINO. I don't really want to comment. I've seen other people make very good conjectures about it being China. I've seen other conjectures as of just being random people. But I don't think it's worth commenting because I'm just not a subject domain expert in intelligence.

Mr. HIGGINS. Intelligence is a safe answer, sir.

When security software is designed, how easy is it for the designer to build a backdoor access that would be virtually undetectable within that cybersecurity software?

Mr. NEINO. We've seen that a multitude of times, and there's very good studies from a variety of areas. The level of entry to do that is very low.

Mr. HIGGINS. Thank you for concluding that.

Brigadier General, my question is to you, sir. Thank you for your service. Are you familiar with Kaspersky Labs out of Moscow?

General TOUHILL. I am familiar with Kaspersky.

Mr. HIGGINS. Manufacturer of cybersecurity products, a long list of cybersecurity products, that top intelligence officials at the FBI, the CIA, the NSA and others advise this body that they don't trust Kaspersky, that they would not use their product on their personal devices. However, it's still used widely across the United States Government in various departments. Can you explain that to this Committee?

General TOUHILL. Well, sir, I don't know what kind of conversation, you know, my colleagues from those agencies had with this Committee. However, as I go and I take a look at the different products that are in the market today, I believe that the American products are the best ones out there, and just on a value proposition, I buy American.

Mr. HIGGINS. I concur. That's a brigadier general speaking right there.

General TOUHILL. That's an American speaking, sir.

Mr. HIGGINS. Let me say that although there's no public evidence of collusion between Kaspersky Labs and the Russian government, it's not a large leap, and Eugene Kaspersky has suggested that his products have no ties to the Russian government. However, as part of the national conversation, Mr. Chairman, and it's widely known that the Russians have been involved in efforts to influence governments across the world with cyber-attack, and Mr. Kaspersky has suggested that he would testify before this body. I strongly suggest that we take him up on his offer. I'd sure like to talk to him regarding the kill switch in North Korea, that having been a rather glaring error on the part of the designer of that worm cyber-attack.

Mr. Neino, what do you think that happened to that guy in North Korea? It was a kill switch, wasn't it? So this message, should it get to any of the cyber-attack cyber experts in North Korea, if you can get out of the country, you're welcome in the West. We'd love to have you before this Committee. We'll give you some real good food.

Mr. Chairman, I yield back.

Chairman LaHood. Thank you, Congressman Higgins.

I now yield to Congresswoman Esty.

Ms. Esty. Thank you very much. This has been very enlightening and extremely helpful.

There are a couple of points I want to return to and maybe drill down on. One is on the human element, which I think is unbelievably important because you can buy all the great equipment in the world, and as you said, Dr. Thompson, if you leave the door open, it doesn't do you any good, and I think a little bit about the analogy in hospitals about getting people used to washing their hands, and it may be low-tech but it works, and so one of the things I think we need to emphasize for all Americans is hygiene. It's just what are proper hygiene practices, so that's one, and getting people's thoughts and how we make that absolutely standard operating procedure for all organizations, government and non-government.

Number two, we have an issue in the federal government in particular at all levels of government of really old systems. So we look at the fact that this was exploiting a vulnerabilities in Windows. Who's still using those systems? Overwhelmingly I can tell you it's local and state governments that don't have any money and they're still using these old systems, so that makes it an even greater issue.

Mr. Neino, your point about threat assessment and understanding levels of assessment, we need triage help. You know, we need triage help to recognize what defcon level is this because, you know, everybody gets those notes on their phones and we're looking at our phones like I don't have time to upgrade my system, and that's the reality of human behavior. So I'd suggest a couple of things. We ought to be getting behavioral economists and social-media experts to your point, Dr. Thompson, and I think that needs to be part of what the federal government, part of what NIST is doing is to stay ahead of the game we need to do that.

A number of us were at an Aspen briefing a couple of months ago with some of the folks from the top levels of the private sector talking about how so much of our emphasis at the federal government has been and frankly the incentives have been for us to be on attack mode. We're developing our attack cyber capability out of the federal government. We've left it to the private sector to do defense. Obviously we need to be doing more defense. So that's—you know, how do we incentivize defense attention? It's less sexy but frankly a lot more important. So what can we do as a culture change? Where does that have to come out of? Is that out of NIST? Is that out of DOD, NSA to put the incentives there? How do we make sure we're getting the broader sector of talent pool.

Again, it may not strike people bringing in, you know, people who do Snapchat for figuring out how do we make sure people don't click on that link but it strikes me over and over again if we don't do that, if we look at what happened in the hacking on the electoral system and last year what happened, it was John Podesta's email where someone clicked on a link, and it is going to be the weakest link and the strongest link at the same time.

So anyone who has thoughts on that whole bunch of stuff I just dumped, that's what happens when you're at the end of the hearing, you know, you're batting clean-up and want to raise a number of issues. But again, thank you very much. I look forward to following with all of you, and thank you for your efforts and in joining with us in figuring out how we can do better for America. Thanks.

Dr. ROMINE. Thank you, Congresswoman. I'll just make two very quick points. One is, we have active research going on now under the program that I just talked about to understand human behavior, trying to understand susceptibility to phishing attacks, and what are the things that factor into people not recognizing that something is a phishing attack. And so there's research coming out about that.

With regard to culture change, I think maybe it's underappreciated sometimes the culture change that's going on in boardrooms and among CEOs who in light of the Framework as a catalyst for this but I think this might have been on their radar anyway, but the Framework is a means of catalyzing the understanding on the part of boardrooms and CEOs that manage risk to reputation, financial risk, and business operational risk and all of the other risks that you're already managing as a CEO, you now have the tools that you can use to incorporate cybersecurity risk into that entire risk management.

General TOUHILL. I'd like to pile onto that. First of all, on the cyber hygiene, we all need to do better, and we work very closely with NIST to help promote the national cyber education programs that we have, and I think we really need to do better on that. As a matter of fact, I propose that we probably need a Woodsy Owl, Smokay the Bear type of thing. You know, I call it Byte. Let's get kids out there fully educated and bring that pipeline up. And we've been working with NIST and across the interagency to do that.

And we also need to incentivize. We shouldn't necessarily be seen as the government that's here to help but not really help but to overregulate. We need to encourage and incentivize folks to do the right thing, to buy down their enterprise risk. But we also have to recognize that risk is an intrinsic part of any management of any business, and we have to be very careful that we don't have hamshackle the different boards and C suites from actually managing their risk, and we need to give them the tools and the support to be good wingmen to help them make those risk decisions.

And then finally, you know, we've had a lot of discussions publicly in this town over the last two, three, four years about roles and missions as to who does what in helping folks. As for me, having served in uniform for over 30 years and then having done some public service on top of that, I think it really takes teamwork, and I view the DOD and NSA and intelligence community's mission to help us with deterrence and interdiction. Let's stop them and take the fight to the bad guys out to foreign shores. But when it comes to protecting hometown America, I believe that that's more appropriate for DHS and the work that's being currently done in the NCCIC to choreograph different activities across the federal government in better serving the citizens.

Mr. THOMPSON. Just a quick comment. First, I support the General's suggest that we resurrect Smokay the Bear. I think it would be great to see him again and maybe kind of repurpose him for this effort. But I will say first, Congresswoman, thank you so much for your comments. I very much agree with what you said about this human element. I can tell you that the practice of security I think is changing very much because of that, and I think about the folks that we hire at Symantec as an example. The kinds of folks that are hunting down the malicious networks today aren't just the computer scientists and mathematicians but there are computational linguists, there are behavioral psychologists, there are anthropologists. There are people that are looking at the human behavior of an attack group, so that's one side.

On the consumer side, which we sell to with Norton, we spend an amazing amount of time thinking about how do we make security similar to the iPad, and I call it the iPad because it's the only piece of technology I think I've ever given to my mom and I didn't have to give her any instruction about how to use it. She just understood it. And we spend a massive amount of time now today on design. How do we make it intuitive? How do we make it easier to be more secure than less secure? And I think that is where a lot of effort must go in in the security community today. How do we make it easier to be more secure than less secure?

Chairman LaHood. Thank you, Congresswoman Esty.

I was just thinking as you referenced Smokay the Bear, maybe a new company, Smokay the Bear Malware would be something——

Mr. Thompson. We'll register the domain, Mr. Chairman.

Chairman LaHood. Thank you.

I now recognize Mr. Palmer for his questions.

Mr. Palmer. Mr. Neino, first, accept our thanks for the quick thinking that allowed the kill switch to prevent so many infections, but with regard to your measurements, however, you suggest that the number of 200,000 infections is too low, and that before the implementation of the kill switch, there may have been 1 to 2 million infections. In that regard, how do you then explain that practically no one tried to pay the ransom if there were that many more?

Mr. Neino. I think there were some who tried to pay the ransom be it the measure of success of that is hard to determine. I think we also——

Mr. Palmer. Well, what you've got is that from many studies that a large portion of the companies do pay the ransoms when their computers are encrypted, but monitoring the Bitcoin wallets advertised in the WannaCry malware, it seems that less than 500 people did, so that's two one-hundredths of 1 percent.

Mr. Neino. Sure. Well, I think——

Mr. Palmer. That's very inconsistent with your——

Mr. Neino. Yeah, I think——

Mr. Palmer. —with what you're saying.

Mr. Neino. I think that when you look at—it's hard to associate the payments to the actual spread, and I'll tell you for a variety of reasons. One, when you look at the actual attack and the magnitude of the attack and you try to trace it to the payment, if you look at the mechanisms to make the payment, it was, one, not clear whether you would get your systems back anyways, and at this point the attacks have been abandoned, so we know that if you pay the ransom, you didn't go anywhere. Most of the media and many of the experts were suggesting not to pay the attack. We were asked the same question and we said you would have to base your own risk organization and determine if you should pay the attack. However, what I can say is the data that we are receiving is absolute. When we get this data—we've been doing this. It's not just WannaCry. We've been doing this for close to a decade. We see and visibly analyze data that comes in. It is accurate.

Mr. PALMER. I'd like to address this question to General Touhill, and again, as many of our members have said, thank you for your service, sir.

Your testimony refers to people who were infected by running Windows 95 but published industry reports are saying that almost everyone that was infected was running Windows 7. So isn't it true that the main reason people were infected was because an intelligence community vulnerability was leaked to the public? Turn on your mic, please.

General TOUHILL. Thanks. Sir, thanks for the question. You know, just for clarity's sake, the—in my written testimony I highlighted Windows 95 as being used as an exemplar. However, there was plenty of other different operating systems that were very susceptible to this type of attack including Windows ME, 7, you know, a lot of unpatched systems.

Mr. PALMER. But I'm asking about an intelligence community vulnerability that was leaked to the public.

General TOUHILL. I think that if we take a look at it from that standpoint, yeah, I'm very concerned about that, and I think that this highlights a couple of things. First of all, patch your systems. We've been telling you all along to do that. Second of all, I think that as we take a look at, you know, the leakage of information or the attribution of leakage of information, that's very serious and unacceptable.

Mr. PALMER. Well, in regard to the patch, the reality is that a team of actors calling themselves shadow brokers published an NSA exploit called EternalBlue on the Internet, and that happened in January 2017, and Microsoft released a patch that addressed that vulnerability 3 months later in March, a patch called MS17–010, so it was not a problem of machines being out of date. The problem was that if you hadn't put all of the Microsoft recommended patches on all the machines within 60 days, you would become a victim, and it was a zero-day attack because when EternalBlue code was released in January, there was no way to protect a computer from it.

General TOUHILL. I don't believe I would characterize this one necessarily as a full-zero-day attack. From my perch, you know, frankly, because the fact that we had some patches that had been put out, and Microsoft went through extraordinary measures, by the way, to go out and create those patches for operating systems that had previously been declared unsupportable many years before, and I use Windows 95 in my written testimony as an exemplar because Windows 95 had been online for about 19 years before it was retired, and for the last three years, Microsoft had not been supporting it, and then for them to come back and put out that patch in March was extraordinary, and through the federal government and other organizations around the world, we went out and we clearly communicated, and Carnegie Mellon's C–CERT was one of them, clearly communicated to all of the communities of interest, patch your systems, this is an important patch, and it was labeled as a critical patch, sir.

Mr. PALMER. If I may, I have one more question for Mr. Thompson. Could you address the double pulsar feature that you mentioned? Since no one was actually paying the ransoms, it is possible that the real goal of the attack was to allow remote access to the machines that the double pulsar was installed on by becoming infected?

Mr. THOMPSON. Thanks for your question. It's difficult to anticipate what the true intention was of this attack, whether it was ransomware, whether it was a test, whether it was the ability to propagate some kind of back door, but what is, I think, interesting as a characteristic of the attack, which I think goes back to your first question of why didn't we see, quote, normal or expected rates of ransomware payment. The backend infrastructure that was set up was very weak compared to the typical piece of ransomware that we see out there in the wild, and it is pretty incredible. Many of these ransomware attacks have a very robust infrastructure behind them. They have almost the equivalent of customer support for people that have been infected with the ransomware. We didn't see that level of sophistication here in the back end.

Mr. PALMER. I thank the witnesses for their answers. I yield back.

Chairman LAHOOD. Thank you, Mr. Palmer.

I now yield to Congressman Webster for his questions.

Mr. WEBSTER. Thank you, Mr. Chairman. Thank for you having this meeting, a joint meeting, and thank each of you for coming, but I'll tell you, my mind has been on something else, and the statements that were given here were similar to that in that they fit. There was an attack yesterday, and I thought about how the fact it was an advanced, persistent threat, and not only that, was it a personalized attack, and there's some people, in fact, my seatmate here, who acted heroically to turn it around, and so I just—that's what was on my mind, these Capitol Police whose service protected life yesterday along with the heroic acts of many of the Members of this Congress. Maybe it's a different kind of threat but it was real, and in this particular case, there was no human error, and so I just—I wanted to take this time that I have, just a few minutes, and say thank you for our people who work there and for the members who serve here who prove there still are heroes in our country and they just haven't been exposed yet, and there was some yesterday that were exposed, so thank you, Mr. Chairman. I yield back.

Chairman LAHOOD. Thank you. I think we have a couple more questions. We're going to go just for a short second round here. I'll yield myself five minutes.

Dr. Romine, you note in your written testimony that the National Vulnerability Database, NVD, that NIST maintains and "updates dozens of times daily" of all known and publicly reported IT vulnerabilities documented that vulnerability that the WannaCry malware exploited. A recent report notes that 75 percent of the vulnerabilities documented last year were disclosed elsewhere first and that it takes on average 7 days between the discovery of a vulnerability and its reporting on the NVD. What is the reason for the delay there if you could talk about that, and is NIST working to get rid of that lag time?

Dr. ROMINE. Thank you for the question. We're always interested in trying to shorten time to deliver really important information to our stakeholders. In the case of NVD, our goal is not first to disclose or first to disseminate the—although we want to do as early as we can. Our real goal is accurate curation, including an assessment of the impact that a vulnerability might have, and that assessment requires a certain amount of analysis that has to be done before we can include something in the National Vulnerability Database.

The other reason for that is that the disclosures are often from sources that are not necessarily reliable from our perspective, and including information about vulnerabilities from sources that we don't view as authoritative would not be in our best interest for the NVD.

Chairman LAHOOD. And was there a delay in reporting the vulnerability that the WannaCry malware exploited?

Dr. ROMINE. I don't know the exact duration between the time that we received the report and the time that we put it in the NVD. I'm sure it was a matter of days.

Chairman LAHOOD. Thank you. Those are all my questions.

I yield to Mr. Beyer.

Mr. BEYER. Thank you, Chairman, very much.

General, you are the first Chief Information Security Officer, and you took that position, I guess, last September under the Obama Administration?

General TOUHILL. Yes, sir.

Mr. BEYER. Do you believe the federal government should have this federal CISO position? I know the Trump Administration hasn't filled it yet, but do you—any reason why you left at the time that you did, and any concerns about whether it will be refilled?

General TOUHILL. Well, first of all, thank you for the question. I believe that this is a best practice to have a Chief Information Security Officer in different organizations. The first Chief Information Security Officer position was created in the private sector over 20 years ago, and it took about 20 years for the federal government to create one. I think it is critically important as part of an enterprise risk management approach that you do in fact have someone who is focused on information security and the risk to the enterprise and advising the corporate community as it were up, down and across as far as what those risks are and best practices to buy down and manage that risk. Within the federal government, we still don't have an authorization for a federal Chief Information Security Officer in statute. My position was appointed as an administrative appointment, and I think that as we take a look at—as we move forward—and the Executive Order that just recently came out is a great step forward. I think we need to firm up and make sure that this position is an enduring position but we also need to authorize and empower the position such that Chief Information Security Officer can in fact have the authorities to choreograph and direct activities that are necessary to better manage our risk.

As far as the appointment goes, I look forward to seeing who the Administration brings forward, and I will coach and serve as wingman for that person.

Mr. BEYER. Great. While we're talking Executive Orders, you made the really interesting case that we overclassify, that the default position right now is to make everything the highest thing, and that we should instead make the default position the lower level of classification and argue our way up. How do we operationalize that? Is this Executive Order, legislation, memorandum of understanding?

General TOUHILL. I thank you for that question. I'm very passionate about it because I was responsible for public and private sector partnerships while I was at DHS and the information sharing between the public sector and the private sector, and frankly, we overclassify too much time-sensitive information in the federal government, in my view, and I believe that the solution set is going to have to be a combination of legislation as well as executive action. So I think that really both branches of government are going to need to partner up as far as—to determine a best means of getting information out faster to folks so that we can timely and actionable actions in this fast-paced cyber environment.

Mr. BEYER. Thank you.

Mr. Neino, you had one very intriguing, or many intriguing lines in your testimony. One said that "points contrary to defense (who did it)" and what I understood from that is we spent too much time trying to figure out who is Lazarus or who is Bayrob rather than defend ourselves. Can you expand on that? Because I confess, as a naturally curious person who watches Law and Order and CSI and all the stuff, I want to know who did it.

Mr. NEINO. I think that the barrier of entry at this point is that anyone could do it, so conjecturing over who has done it is a very difficult task because cybersecurity is something that could be easily misdirected. You never really know who the attack is, and focusing on that doesn't solve the problem that we're vulnerable. We are vulnerable. So if you leave the door open, there could be thousands of people that walk by your house every day. Would it really matter if it's because you leave yourself exposed who has done it? They do it because they can, and we should not make it that way. We should make it so that we are resilient and we are a very strong nation in regards to defense.

Mr. BEYER. Thank you.

Dr. Thompson, do you want to pile on at all?

Mr. THOMPSON. I do. Thank you. You know, it's interesting. We don't spend very much time looking at who did it and who is the country behind it, who is the enterprise behind it, who is the person behind it, but it's very critical for us to associate patterns of behavior. So if we associate attack A with attack B and then believe that these two things are connected, it will let us learn more about that group, the tactics that they use, and make is better prepared to protect against a new attack sight unseen, and that was the case with Symantec's AV engines and our artificial intelligence engines because of previous training on this against the WannaCry malware. So it's critical for us to have that grouping together and we'll leave it up to the intelligence community to decide who that group actually belongs to.

Mr. BEYER. Great. Thank you very much, Mr. Chair.

Chairman LaHood. Mr. Lipinski, do you have any follow-up questions?

Mr. LIPINSKI. No, I think I took plenty of time on my first round. I thank the witnesses for your testimony, all the work. As I said, I'm sure we'll be continuing this discussion, so thank you.

Chairman LaHood. In closing, I want to thank all of the witnesses here today for your important, insightful and impactful testimony here today, and as our two Subcommittees look at legislation and public policy as it relates to cybersecurity and the ancillary issues of national security, economic vulnerabilities, privacy, we look forward to continuing to work with you on those issues and appreciate you taking time out of your busy schedule to be here today.

And the record will remain open for two weeks for additional written comments and written questions from Members, and at this time the hearing is adjourned.

[Whereupon, at 11:51 a.m., the Subcommittees were adjourned.]

Appendix I

ANSWERS TO POST-HEARING QUESTIONS

Responses by Dr. Charles H. Romine
U.S. HOUSE OF REPRESENTATIVES
COMMITTEE ON SCIENCE, SPACE, AND TECHNOLOGY
Subcommittee on Oversight
Subcommittee on Research and Technology

Hearing Questions for the Record
The Honorable Roger Marshall (R-KS)

Bolstering the Government's Cybersecurity: Lessons Learned from WannaCry

Questions for Dr. Romine

---

1. What key lessons can the government and the private sector learn in the aftermath of the WannaCry attack, to better prevent these attacks from happening in the future?

<u>NIST RESPONSE</u>:

Key lessons learned in the aftermath of the WannaCry attack are that some critical actions are needed to prevent or limit damage from cyberattacks. These actions include:

1) migrating from unsupported operating systems and software;

2) patching and maintaining technologies used in operating environments; and

3) implementing and periodically testing response and recovery procedures and systems.

Another important lesson is that it is critically important to develop active public-private collaboration and coordination to successfully prepare for, respond to, and recover from current and future attacks.

NIST provides resources to assist organizations in preventing or, at least, quickly recovering from ransomware attacks with trust that the recovered data is accurate, complete, and free of malware and that the recovered system is trustworthy and capable.

To better prevent ransomware attacks, the government and the private sector can follow the voluntary standards, guidelines, and practices outlined in the Framework for Improving Critical Infrastructure Cybersecurity. This document reinforces the importance of capabilities necessary to respond to, and recover from, cybersecurity attacks.

In the case of WannaCry and similar ransomware, the Framework helps organizations understand and manage cybersecurity risk and reinforces the importance of capabilities used to respond to, and recover from ransomware attacks. For example, the Framework identifies network monitoring to "detect potential cybersecurity events," including the presence of "malicious code," and to compare them to "expected data flows" in the network to help organizations quickly detect and contain the malicious code and to determine the effectiveness of eradication measures. While the Framework allows an organization to determine its priorities based on its risk tolerance, it also prompts a sequence of interrelated cybersecurity risk management decisions, which should prevent virus infection and propagation and support expeditious response and recovery activities. To support greater integration of cybersecurity into all organizational operations, NIST has also produced the <u>Baldrige Cybersecurity Excellence Builder</u> (BCEB), a Framework-aligned self-assessment tool that seeks to help organizations improve the effectiveness of their cybersecurity risk management efforts across cybersecurity activities included in the Framework.

Also, the Federal government and others can use guidance provided in a draft interagency report (NISTIR 8170), *The Cybersecurity Framework: Implementation Guidance for Federal Agencies.* Available at http://csrc.nist.gov/publications/drafts/nistir-8170/nistir8170-draft.pdf. This report illustrates eight use cases in which Federal agencies can leverage the Framework to address common cybersecurity-related responsibilities. By doing so, agencies can integrate the Framework with key NIST cybersecurity risk-management standards and guidelines already in wide use at various organizational levels. The goal of these efforts is to allow Federal agencies to build more robust and mature agency-wide cybersecurity risk management programs.

To recover from cyberattacks – including ransomware attacks – the government and the private sector can develop an actionable set of steps, described in NIST's Guide for Cybersecurity Event Recovery, that focus on a unique type of cyber-event and can be tailored to fit the dependencies of the people, processes, and technologies of a specific organization.

NIST recently initiated a project at our National Cybersecurity Center of Excellence (NCCoE) on data integrity, specifically focused on recovering from cyberattacks. This project will enable organizations to answer questions such as: "What data was corrupted?"; "When was the data corrupted?"; "How was the data corrupted?"; and "Who corrupted the data?". Organizations will be able to use the results of NCCoE's research to recover trusted backups, roll back data to a known good state, alert administrators when there is a change to a critical system, and restore services quickly after a WannaCry-like cyberattack.

Another NIST resource that can assist system administrators in protecting against cyberattacks such as the WannaCry ransomware is the most recent release of the NIST National Software Reference Library (NSRL). The NSRL provides a collection of software from various sources and unique file profiles, which is most often used by law enforcement, government, and industry organizations to review files on a computer by matching file profiles in the system.

In addition to the NSRL, NIST also provides a repository of all known and publicly reported IT vulnerabilities, such as the one exploited by the WannaCry malware. The repository, called the National Vulnerability Database (NVD), is an authoritative source of standardized information on security vulnerabilities that NIST updates dozens of times daily. The NVD is used by security vendors as well as tools and service providers around the world to help them identify whether they have vulnerabilities. For example, the WannaCry malware exploited a vulnerability that was well documented in the NVD database. Organizations that use the NVD database to identify and address their computer systems' vulnerabilities can better prepare against malware that exploit these vulnerabilities. The patch issued by Microsoft on March 14 was meant to remove such vulnerabilities and allowed computer systems to be protected from the WannaCry malware attack.

Responses by Mr. Gregory J. Touhill

U.S. HOUSE OF REPRESENTATIVES
COMMITTEE ON SCIENCE, SPACE, AND TECHNOLOGY
Subcommittee on Oversight
Subcommittee on Research and Technology

Hearing Questions for the Record
The Honorable Roger Marshall (R-KS)

Bolstering the Government's Cybersecurity: Lessons Learned from WannaCry
Questions for Mr. Touhill

1. **Kansas State University's Cyber Defense Club has earned top-tier recognition from Argonne National Laboratory, and Friends University, located in Wichita, Kansas, recently launched a graduate program in cyber security that will prepare graduates to be on the front line of defense.**

   Could you touch on the vital role universities play in preparing our future against these attacks?

Mr. Touhill: Thank you for the question. Cybersecurity is a risk management issue, not just a technology problem and universities are an essential element in preparing our up-and-coming work force to better manage cyber risk.

Great universities, such as Carnegie Mellon, contribute in many ways to help society better manage cyber risk.

First, they expose students to basic training on existing concepts, tools, systems, and procedures. The students are introduced to the state-of-the-art. Training helps the students understand the "what and how" behind what is considered state-of-the-art or what the technology world often calls, "best practice". When it comes to cybersecurity, following best practices is an essential element of a successful risk management program and part of a due care, due diligence program.

Secondly, universities educate and encourage students to explore different concepts, question the status quo, uncover new solutions, and discover the future. Education doesn't just guide the students on the "what and how", it helps the student discover "why". The education universities provide our students prepares the next generation of citizens to be more cyber aware. It prepares them to be more inquisitive, adaptive, and innovative as they create and embrace new technologies. The training and education we provide also helps our students become more responsible citizens as they understand the evolving ethical and societal norms spawned by Internet-enabled technology. Not only do our graduates emerge from our classrooms better prepared in their chosen field of study, they are better prepared for the world around them. They are cyber aware.

Thirdly, our universities prepare our students to discover tomorrow. Through research and development activities, which this committee and other government entities so generously contribute, our university and others guide our students to challenge the status quo and active pursue solutions to previously unsolvable problems. We explore new ideas, create new materials, invent new products, and find new cures. We inspire the next generation of scientists, business professionals, artists, engineers, and doctors who will change the world. Our laboratories are not just placed of discovering new inventions, they are places where our students discover themselves. I am convinced that the next huge step in cybersecurity technology will be conceived in a university lab.

2. **What key lessons can the government and the private sector learn in the aftermath of the WannaCry attack, to better prevent these attacks from happening in the future?**

Mr. Touhill: I believe that attacks like these will indeed occur in the future yet we can learn from our experience during the WannaCry attack to minimize the negative impacts and better manage our cyber risk.

First, cybersecurity professionals like myself have been promoting adoption of best practices as a matter of "due care and due diligence". Best practices articulated by the United States Computer Emergency Readiness Team (US-CERT) include:

- Lockdown your log-in with multi-factor authentication
- "Don't put all your eggs in one basket": Segment your network
- Implement Whitelisting so unauthorized code doesn't run on your system
- Keep your computer and software up-to-date; install the latest patches

The way the WannaCry software was engineered, the most vulnerable victims were those who were operating computer systems with antique, out-dated, or unpatched software. Had the victims been following best practices, they would have reduced their vulnerabilities and, arguably, a properly patched and configured machine would have thwarted the attack.

Secondly, we have to acknowledge that determined adversaries are going to try to attack again. In my testimony I stated that WannaCry was like a slow-pitched softball while I believe future attacks will come in like a high-and-tight fastball. I still believe that. Because there will be more attacks, I believe we need to pay closer attention to treating cybersecurity as an enterprise risk issue.

When it comes to managing your cyber risk, I like to use the National Cyber Risk Framework to help structure my cyber risk management program. Frameworks are formal methodologies used to address issues. Our National Cyber Risk Framework helps focus risk managers and decision makers to:

- <u>Identify</u> their assets (and information indeed is an asset) as well as the threats to those assets
- <u>Protect</u> against those threats based on the enterprise risk appetite
- <u>Detect</u> when the assets are at risk from attack or outside of normal operations
- <u>Respond</u> appropriately when under attack or outside of normal operations
- <u>Recover</u> quickly and completely because resiliency has been built in

I am a proponent of the National Cyber Risk Framework and I am grateful to this committee for promoting it. I encourage the committee to formally designate what some call the NIST Cyber Risk Framework as the <u>National</u> Cyber Risk Framework.

Responses by Dr. Hugh Thompson

U.S. HOUSE OF REPRESENTATIVES
COMMITTEE ON SCIENCE, SPACE, AND TECHNOLOGY
Subcommittee on Oversight
Subcommittee on Research and Technology

Hearing Questions for the Record
The Honorable Roger Marshall (R-KS)

Bolstering the Government's Cybersecurity: Lessons Learned from WannaCry

Questions for Dr. Thompson

---

1. **What key lessons can the government and the private sector learn in the aftermath of the WannaCry attack, to better prevent these attacks from happening in the future?**

WannaCry outbreak stopped before it caused major global, damage, but this was as much through good fortune as it was through what was a largely effective response. Learning the lessons of WannaCry and improving our ability to respond is essential, because another attack is always coming. In fact, less than two weeks after this hearing, there was another global outbreak called Petya. Like WannaCry, Petya was a self-propagating worm, and at first glance appeared to be ransomware. But unlike WannaCry, Petya was designed primarily to overwrite data – effectively destroying it – rather than to encrypt it. Because of the files it attacked, Petya destroyed most of the computers it infected.

One lesson that can be learned from these outbreaks is simply that they will continue. Agencies need to closely monitor system vulnerabilities, fully deploy modern security tools, and keep their patches up-to-date. WannaCry was not a "zero-day" exploit so effective patch management would have protected users, as appears to have been the case with US government systems. But even on unpatched systems, or legacy systems, Symantec's security tools detected and blocked all but a handful of WannaCry infection attempts. Deploying modern security software, and ensuring that it is properly employed, is essential if we are going to keep pace with sophisticated adversaries.

Another lesson is the importance of an effective response. WannaCry was not the first major cyber incident industry and government have worked on together, and that was reflected by the coordinated response. The US government reacted quickly to the outbreak, and worked well with industry experts. DHS's National Cybersecurity and Communications Integration Center (NCCIC) held twice-daily calls with the private sector to coordinate operational activities. Symantec participated, as did more than a dozen security and IT companies. During these calls, DHS representatives and the private sector shared Indicators of Compromise (IoCs), mitigation techniques, and information on threat vectors. In addition, the NCCIC distributed written analysis on the attack. Symantec worked closely with the US government from the first hours of the outbreak. We connected DHS researchers with our experts, provided IoCs and analysis to DHS, and received the same from DHS. After the infection waned, we continued our partnership, sharing details about the Lazarus connections (detailed below) that that we were finding. From our perspective, this was one of the most successful public/private incident response efforts in which we have participated.

Appendix II

Additional Material for the Record

STATEMENT SUBMITTED BY FULL COMMITTEE
RANKING MEMBER EDDIE BERNICE JOHNSON

<u>OPENING STATEMENT</u>
Ranking Member Eddie Bernice Johnson (D-TX)

House Committee on Science, Space, and Technology
Subcommittee on Oversight
Subcommittee on Research & Technology
"Bolstering the Government's Cybersecurity: Lessons Learned from WannaCry,"
June 15, 2017

Thank you Chairman LaHood and Chairwoman Comstock.

As I have said many times on this subject before, cybersecurity is a difficult threat to confront. It is continually evolving and constantly presenting serious dangers to our personal and national security. Every time you pick up a newspaper, it is apparent that no one is safe from these threats. Cybersecurity weapons can compromise our government systems, financial systems, healthcare services, electric power grid, sensitive private information, and even our voting systems – the very lifeblood of our democracy.

Although some cybersecurity threats are highly sophisticated, backed by well-trained foreign actors and nation states, even crudely developed cyber threats can be successful because they rely on the flaws and vulnerabilities of unsuspecting human beings to help launch penetrations of digital networks.

Personal, private sector, and federal government vigilance is key to confronting this threat. A 22-year-old cybersecurity analyst employed by Kryptos Logic helped derail the recent Ransomware attack resulting from the WannaCry virus because he acted quickly. That is one lesson learned from the WannaCry attack. Another lesson is the importance of quickly implementing security patches issued by software providers. U.S. government and private sector systems were largely immune to WannaCry because our systems managers did just that.

Like many other cyber threats, the success of WannaCry was dependent on individuals inadvertently helping it infect computers and proliferate. Those who are simply users of digital technology today, which includes all of us, our children and grandchildren alike, should all heed these lessons. Empowering individuals to take appropriate precautions against the wide-range of current and emerging cyber threats and encouraging them to remain vigilant in both the work place and at home is one of our best defenses. People are critical to ensuring our cyber-security. The best technical tools in the world won't do much good when individuals mistakenly open the door to these digital dangers.

I look forward to the testimony of our witnesses. I would also like to thank retired Brigadier General Gregory Touhill for being here today. He has had a long career in cybersecurity. He was a deputy assistant secretary for cybersecurity and communications at DHS and was appointed as the first federal Computer Information Security Officer (CISO) last September, a position he left in January of this year. Gen. Touhill is currently an Adjunct Professor of Cybersecurity & Risk Management at Carnegie Mellon University.

Thank you General Touhill and all of our witnesses for testifying today.

Thank you Mr. Chairman. I yield back.

www.ingramcontent.com/pod-product-compliance
Lightning Source LLC
Chambersburg PA
CBHW081314250726

48662CB00008B/2563